Herbert Elliott Hamblen

The General Manager's Story

Old-Time Reminiscences of Railroading in the United States

Herbert Elliott Hamblen

The General Manager's Story
Old-Time Reminiscences of Railroading in the United States

ISBN/EAN: 9783744677738

Printed in Europe, USA, Canada, Australia, Japan

Cover: Foto ©ninafisch / pixelio.de

More available books at **www.hansebooks.com**

THE GENERAL MANAGER'S STORY

"And then I swept by like a cyclone." — See p. 158.

Frontispiece.

THE
GENERAL MANAGER'S STORY

OLD-TIME REMINISCENCES OF RAILROADING
IN THE UNITED STATES

BY

HERBERT ELLIOTT HAMBLEN

AUTHOR OF "ON MANY SEAS"

New York
THE MACMILLAN COMPANY
LONDON: MACMILLAN & CO., Ltd.
1898

Norwood Press
J. S. Cushing & Co. – Berwick & Smith
Norwood Mass. U.S.A.

To

THE RAILROAD MEN OF THE UNITED STATES

CONTENTS

	PAGE
INTRODUCTION	1

CHAPTER I
LEAVES HOME	5

CHAPTER II
LEARNING TO JUMP	11

CHAPTER III
BREAKING IN	26

CHAPTER IV
A CLEVER TRICK	36

CHAPTER V
A MISTAKE IN ORDER	46

CHAPTER VI
A RAILROAD AUTOCRAT	59

CHAPTER VII
CATCHES A TARTAR	70

CHAPTER VIII
PROMOTED TO THE LEFT SIDE	85

CONTENTS

CHAPTER IX
Chasing a Run-away 109

CHAPTER X
At the Throttle 131

CHAPTER XI
In the Nick of Time 151

CHAPTER XII
Fifty-two Hours on Duty 174

CHAPTER XIII
A Ten Per Cent Cut 200

CHAPTER XIV
We strike 218

CHAPTER XV
Joys of Tramping 236

CHAPTER XVI
Sons of Rest 249

CHAPTER XVII
Hired again 266

CHAPTER XVIII
I lose my Nerve 281

CHAPTER XIX
My Turn at Last 299

LIST OF ILLUSTRATIONS

"And then I swept by like a cyclone" (p. 158) . *Frontispiece*

	FACING PAGE
"It was certainly a high jump"	20
"I delighted in catching and riding on the most swiftly flying cars"	32
"I watch that grimy left hand on the throttle" . . .	41
"Her engineer shouted something that we couldn't catch"	44
"They met exactly under the bridge"	48
"It wasn't long before I crawled under the truck" . .	53
"'Mr. Grinnell, your engine truck centre casting is broken all to pieces'"	83
"We found the gentleman sitting with his feet cocked up on his desk, smoking"	99
"'You've forced yourself on here where you're not wanted'"	116
"We found grooves nearly a quarter of an inch deep" .	141
"She was a beautiful sight! No stack, no pilot, no head lamp"	144
"'Section foreman's got a rail up'"	152
"And now I saw ahead of me a man in the middle of the track"	156

LIST OF ILLUSTRATIONS

	FACING PAGE
"Looked along the barrel of a big revolver"	200
"The wrecking train was hardly ever idle"	204
"'Sa-ay! you've nominated about everybody'"	216
"The clerks in the offices were hustled out into the yard"	232
"The night shut down on a dreary scene of smoking desolation"	234
Roundhouse Studies	266
"He nearly squelched the breath out of my body"	297

THE GENERAL MANAGER'S STORY

INTRODUCTION

"Do I remember my first day's railroading? Indeed I do, my boy, although it was nearly forty years ago. Yes, I remember it, and every day's railroading I have done since." The speaker was General Manager M—— of a great railroad system branching out from Chicago, the lines of which form the connecting link between that great metropolis and hundreds of cities and towns far away on the prairies, or among the mountains, giving employment to thousands of men, and furnishing the means of transportation to thousands more. Mr. M——, who had been a lifelong friend of my father, was a fine old gentleman, with a ruddy, jovial countenance, kindly blue eyes, and I think the most beautiful silvery hair I have ever seen.

When he grasped your hand, and bade you welcome, and asked what he could do for you, as he had done to me the previous evening, on my arrival at his summer home, away up in the glorious mountains of Nevada, you felt a thrill as of a gentle electric shock go through your veins, and your heart went out to the old gentleman at once.

I knew from my father that Mr. M—— was a self-made man, and had worked his way up from the very lowest station of railroad life by sheer force of indomitable will, perseverance, and fidelity to duty, until he was then the sole guiding spirit in the operation of thousands of miles of a great American railroad system, — a position which calls for great managerial ability.

He who would hold such an immense system in the hollow of his hand, as it were, must be capable of quick thought in an emergency, keen and absolutely correct judgment, — for mistakes in railroading are costly investments, — and a knowledge of the business in its minutest details that is almost marvellous to contemplate.

How little does the average passenger realize, when he steps on the sumptuously furnished car, and quietly reads the newspaper, until the brakeman calls out his station, and he steps off to go to his family, or his business, that his train has been under the keen supervision of an army of trained officials and employees during every minute of its progress; that its arrival at, and departure from, each station has been ticked over the wire to the train despatcher; that all meeting-points with other trains have been carefully prepared for; that rules and orders have been issued providing for every possible contingency; that, in fact, as an old railroad man said to me once, "If everybody obeyed orders, collisions would be possible only when brought about by unavoidable accidents."

These men are carefully chosen, and only long and faithful service, a strictly first-class moral character, and undoubted ability to perform the duties of the position, will insure their promotion to the higher offices, or their retention in them.

Promotion on a railroad is slow, and for merit only.

At the head of this band of experts, over the superintendents, stands the General Manager, a walking epitome of railroad knowledge. Tried by many years of service in minor positions and proved trustworthy in all, he is the one chosen from many as the best fitted for this responsible position.

As I looked at the old gentleman sitting there so comfortably in his big rush-bottomed rocking-chair, lazily blowing the smoke from his "perfecto" out into the cool starlight, the personification of ease and wealth, I found it hard to believe that those plump, rosy palms had ever been calloused by contact with the iron brake-wheel, or the fireman's scoop-shovel; but I knew they had, and I knew too that even now he would not hesitate a moment to leave his luxurious home and go out in the stormiest night to a wreck, to render such assistance as his ripe experience in all branches of the service eminently fitted him to give.

I had arrived in answer to a cordial invitation to

pass my vacation with him in his summer eyrie halfway up the mountain side.

Born and brought up in a small railroad town, I had always been an ardent though bashful admirer of the grimy-visaged, weather-beaten fellows who, night and day, in darkness, fog, and storm, speed fearlessly over the glistening steel rails to their journey's end, or down to death, as their fate may determine.

So, when I found myself placed in such extremely favorable circumstances for obtaining a fund of genuine railroad lore, I was bound to improve the opportunity, and gradually drew out from my veteran friend the story which follows, and which I shall tell as nearly as possible in his own words, hoping that it may prove as interesting to the reader as it did to me.

CHAPTER I

HIS EARLY LIFE AT HOME — HE BECOMES ENAMOURED OF THE RAILROAD — SEES A TRAIN BREAK IN TWO ON A HEAVY GRADE — NEGLECTS HIS STUDIES TO WATCH AND ADMIRE THE TRAINS — FAILS IN HIS EXAMINATIONS AT THE ACADEMY AND LEAVES IN DISGRACE — TAKING THE FIRST TRAIN OUT OF TOWN

My father was a stern puritanical clergyman, who considered a smile on the Sabbath to be a sin, and a hearty laugh, even on a week day, a grievous breach of decorum; and as I was always of an exceedingly mirthful disposition, I was almost constantly under the ban of parental displeasure, and through some innate depravity of my nature, I suppose, I always felt an aversion to any line of business that would compel me to be always studying the proprieties of dress and manners. I felt a sort of good-natured contempt for my companions in the village academy, who looked forward to a position in a bank as the most desirable opening to be had, while I longed for a life in the open air, without too many refinements, even with a dash of roughness in it, and if with a spice of adventure or danger, all the better.

Our home was so situated that it overlooked a long

heavy grade on the local railroad, and I used frequently to watch with the greatest interest the freight trains as they slowly and laboriously puffed and tugged up the hill, the brakemen sitting — if it happened to be pleasant weather — on their brake-wheels, with folded arms, and hat brims flapping in the breeze, monarchs of all they surveyed. Sometimes they would, for some cause at that time unknown to me, stop on a slight curve nearly in front of our place, and then there would be a great shouting and waving of arms and hats. Sometimes the conductor would come up over the top of the train, and jaw at the engineer, who apparently never failed to give him fully as good as he sent; then if they failed to start again, they would cut the train in two in the middle, and take half of it up at a time, to a convenient side-track at the top, where it would be coupled together again and proceed on its way.

But it was on the down trips that I got excited. As soon as the engine pitched over the hill with cars enough to keep up the speed, the engineer would shut off his steam, and the train, gathering headway from its own weight, would whirl down the grade at a great rate. The engineer would blow his whistle, and the brakemen, running lightly over the tops of the bounding and rocking cars, that seemed every minute as if they must leave the tracks and pile themselves in the ditch, would twist up the brakes with a vim as though they would tear them out by the roots — and oh! how I admired them then! What a glorious thing it must be, I thought, to feel within one's self the courage and self-reliance necessary to enable one to speed over the top of that reeling train, and, as it were, tame it in its wild flight, and bring it under control, or to a perfect standstill. Yes, my boy, there's poetry even in a freight brakeman's life, though you mightn't think it.

There was one fellow — I remember him as well as if it had been but yesterday, — a big, tall, strapping man — a perfect Hercules. He always rode out near the middle of the train when going down the hill, and I fancied that I could see the train perceptibly slow up every time that he set a brake. One day his train broke in two a couple of cars ahead of where he sat. I noticed a gradually widening gap between the cars, and he soon spied it too; for he leaped to his feet, let a wild yell out of him to attract the engineer's attention, pulled off his straw hat, and swung it in a full-arm vertical circle in front of him, and having thus signalled the engineer, commenced to set brakes with all his might; for you see when a train breaks in two on a down grade, the first result is, that the head section draws away from the rear one; but as it is pushing the locomotive with all its machinery, the rear section, unless checked by the brakes, will gain in speed so much faster that it will crash into it, resulting in some of the worst wrecks known to railroad men. When the engineer gets a signal that his train is broken in two, or discovers the fact himself, by looking back on a curve, he instantly "pulls out" and runs as fast as possible to get away from the rear section, at the same time giving the whistle signal for "broke in two," to notify the train crew, so that they can get out and stop their end.

Well, it seems that in this case the engineer either saw the head brakeman signal or discovered the break himself, for I saw the head end dart away, and heard four long blasts of the whistle repeated again and again. The train men responded promptly and did their level best to stop their half; but the hill was so steep and the train had got such headway on it, and so quickly, that even with all brakes set, and the fire flying from the wheels in showers, they went down that grade like a stone dropping down a well. I had an unobstructed view of the track for several miles, and watched with the keenest interest this novel race. At first it seemed as if the locomotive gained quite rapidly, and by the volumes of black smoke pouring out of her stack I knew that the engineer was giving it to her for all she was worth. After awhile she seemed barely to hold her own, and then the rear section seemed to gain on the one ahead; but as they were now well down the road, this might have been partly due to perspective. Anyway, I saw that they finally got the rear part stopped; the engine, that had now got half a mile or more away from them, backed up on getting a signal, coupled on, and away they went.

This incident — which, as I afterwards learned,

was a very common occurrence — so fired my imagination from the heroism of the big brakeman, whose prompt action had prevented a wreck with the consequent loss of thousands of dollars' worth of property, and very likely some human lives, that I determined to devote my life to railroading. I lost all interest in my studies, could fix my mind on nothing, and passed all my spare time, and a good deal that I could not afford to spare, in watching the trains, and constructing in imagination wonderful cases of lives and property saved by my individual prowess *when* I should become a railroad man.

Shortly after this our annual examination came off at the academy, and as I had neglected my studies of late, I failed wofully. My father was a sorely disappointed man, and notified me in very plain terms that he could not afford to keep me another year at school, and as I had — so he said — disgraced him by my miserable failure, he would be pleased if I could find some occupation, at least for awhile, away from my native place. In conclusion he handed me two ten-dollar bills, saying, that while he could not spare me any more just at present, he did not wish a son of his to be short of anything that a young man in my station ought to have, and told me in case I failed to obtain satisfactory employment before my money was gone, not to hesitate about writing for more, or coming home again in case I failed to find any employment at all, which he broadly hinted he expected would be the case, as I had already begun life so disastrously.

You may well believe that this lecture was quite a set-back to me, for I had certainly not contemplated anything so harsh as what was really neither more nor less than being turned out of doors. I was proud and stubborn, however, so I thanked him kindly for the money, and told him I guessed I could hoe my own row all right, to which he replied stiffly, "I presume so," and asked me if I had any plans for the future which I cared to confide to him. I answered just as stiffly, "None at all, sir," and left his presence forever. I had a tearful scene with mother and the girls, and declining their earnest entreaties to remain in the house at least until morning, I packed a small valise and took the first train out of town.

CHAPTER II

HE ARRIVES LATE AT NIGHT AT THE JUNCTION — SEEKING EMPLOYMENT — FALLS INTO STRANGE ADVENTURES — IS HAZED BY A VETERAN BRAKEMAN — HEARS DISCOURAGING TALES — TAKES LESSONS — LEARNING TO JUMP — YARDMASTER'S ADVICE — DEATH IN THE YARD — HIRED

As I had never before been ten miles from the house I was born in, the novelty of the train ride served to distract my mind from dwelling too much on my unpleasant condition. Besides, as I had fully made up my mind to enter the railroad service, I took a great interest in all I saw pertaining to the business; and when the conductor, a little, wiry, quick, nervous old fellow, with a long gray beard, and gorgeous in blue cloth, brass buttons, and a shiny badge, came through the train, I with difficulty repressed my desire to confide in him my mission on earth. But he had a cold, fishy eye, so he escaped.

We arrived at eleven o'clock at night at the end of our run, which I found next day to be a junction with a large road whose western terminus was at Chicago. I put up at a hotel near the station, and after breakfast the next morning, made my way down to the railroad yard, which I could see quite plainly from the hotel piazza.

The sound of the switch engines as they puffed to and fro, and the bang and rattle of the cars as they were rammed together, was music to me, and served to strengthen my resolution to become a railroad man. That I might not find employment never occurred to me; for being so perfectly and beautifully green, I didn't know there was in existence an art called "hunting a job." So it was with a rather benign and philanthropic feeling that I slowly wandered down there, and stood for some time watching the flying cars, and wondering what was accomplished by the work I saw in progress, for to me it seemed to be entirely aimless. An engine would back into a track, couple on, and then after dragging the cars out, would kick them all over the yard, only to go to another track and do the same thing over again, while other engines would take the cars she had kicked and distribute them elsewhere.

After watching them for nearly an hour, and failing to discover what their object was, I walked along towards the other end of the yard, where I came across an old man with a wooden leg, who was trimming switch lamps. I watched him awhile, and as he appeared to have plenty of time, I stepped up to him, and raising my hat politely, said,—

"Good morning, sir."

He looked at me in a surprised manner, and then after looking everywhere else, came to the conclusion, apparently, that it must have been himself that I addressed, as he could see no one else. So he replied rather sheepishly, though in a not unfriendly manner, —

"Good mornin'."

"This is a fine railroad you have here, sir," said I.

"Yas, on'y 'tain't mine," said he; "b'longs mostly ter the comp'ny, I guess."

I told him I knew that, of course, asked him what road it was, and what was the proper way to obtain employment there.

He sized me up with a quick, comprehensive glance, and said they could tell me all about that in the office, but I told him I didn't want to work in the office, I wanted to work on the cars.

Just then another old fellow came up. He had only one eye, and a terrible scar ran diagonally across his face from eyebrow to chin. This had crushed and distorted his nose, drawn one corner of his left eye down, and the opposite corner of his mouth up, thereby showing a couple of filthy, tobacco-stained tusks, and giving him the most repulsive appearance of any human being I ever saw.

His overalls were black with dirt, and so shiny with grease that when the sun shone on him he glistened like a crow. His left arm was cut off just below the elbow, and finished out with a three-pronged iron hook, in which he carried a great iron pail filled with colored cotton waste soaked in oil.

In his right and only hand he had what I took to be a mammoth coffee-pot, but which was in reality an oil-can.

When I first caught sight of his horrible features I was startled, but the distortion at the corner of his mouth caused me to think that he was trying to smile a welcome, so again I lifted my hat, and bade him good morning; but without taking the slightest notice of me, he stepped up to a box car, set his load down on the ground, lifted the cover of an axle-box with his hook, thrust it in, and pulling out a lot of dry black waste, turned to my friend the lamp-trimmer, and holding it up, said, —

"Looker that, Joe; d'ye ever see the way these furrin cars comes inter the yard now'days? Dry's a powder horn; no wonder they burn off journals, an' break down, an' block the road. Since ole Beeswax died, 'n' they got that blasted young clerk in here fer yardmaster, everything's gone to the devil. The first thing he does is to cut down the caboose supplies, till not one conductor out o' three's got a dope bucket; an' then I have ter cart a carload o' dope round the yard every day, 'n' it all comes o' puttin' boys that don't know nothin' about practical railroadin' over men that furgits more every night than they'll ever know. Ter blazes with sich dam-fool management, I say," and he fired the kiln-dried waste on the ground in disgust, and commenced vigorously ramming in a lot of the mixture from his pail which he called "dope," all the time swearing away and wondering what "ole Beeswax" would say if he could see how things were being run into the ground and destroyed by his unworthy successor.

"Why, Mike," said the lamp-trimmer, "here's a man for you," indicating me by a sort of jerk of the head, which enabled him to point towards me with the old clay pipe he was affectionately sucking.

"Man for who? What do I want of a man? Guess yer gittin' loony," said Mike.

"Why, didn't I hear you say last night that you wanted another brakeman? He wants to learn to be a brakeman."

"Oh!" said Mike, stopping his work at once and leaning lazily up against the side of the car, while his disfigured features assumed a different expression, which I presume indicated interest. "So ye want to learn to be a brakeman, boy? What road are ye off of? Ben a water boy, I s'pose?"

I told him I had never worked anywhere yet; was, in fact, just from school.

"Well, I'll tell ye what you do now, sonny: you jest run right back to school an' keep away from the railroad; 'tain't no good. I've been a brakeman twenty-seven years; so's Joe there. See this patent safety coupler?" (holding up his hook); "got that brakin'. Conductor said if I couldn't couple cars when they was comin' together quicker 'n chain lightnin', I'd better hunt another job, in a dry-goods store or somethin'. Wish't I had now; might o' had *two* old-fashioned couplers yet instid of on'y one an' this thing.

"Tried to make one o' them flyin' couplin's not twenty minutes afterwards; drawhead mashed into a rotten car, an' I jumped back jest in time to keep from gittin' squ'shed when they come together, but got my arm cut off.

"See this beauty mark on my mug like a single-track switchback up the side of a mountain? Got throwed off o' the top of a car in a head'n'head collision, an' ploughed down the side of a forty-foot rock fill on my nose. That's railroadin'!

"Ask Joe there why he don't wear his other leg every day like most folks? Cos ole Bill Herndon that was killed in the big wreck at Jenkins' Trestle four year ago flew a flat car over 'im one day an' cut it off — that's why."

"I have always lived near the railroad," said I, "and I never saw any brakeman who had been maimed like you two gentlemen. I think you must have had exceptionally bad luck."

"'Cepshunally bad luck? 'cepshunally *good* luck, you mean. We hain't neither of us killed yet, be we? Where do you s'pose the rest of the fellers is that went brakin' when we did? Killed, every mother's son of 'em, years an' years ago.

"We're both on us nigher sixty 'n fifty. You don't see but mighty few brakeys as old as we be, now I tell ye.

"The reason you didn't see no cripples on the

trains is 'cos they don't send 'em out on the road; 'tain't likely. What good 'd they be? Them's all fresh fish that you saw. Ain't ben at the business long; but they'll git it, you'll see. What 're brakemen for, anyway? Nothin' but fodder for cars 'n' engines to eat up. Say, do you want to go brakin'?"

I was on my mettle, and determined not to let the old fellow think he had scared me by his tirade; so I said yes I did.

"Wal, I want another man, 'n' you look to be a pretty lively young feller, but you're so awful green. It'd cost me more to break ye in nor ye'd be worth for a month ter come," and he looked at me with his eyes half shut, a cunning leer showing in spite of his bisected countenance.

It flashed suddenly on my mind that perhaps if I should offer to pay him for his trouble it might simplify matters, so I said, "I know of course that I am green, but I wouldn't mind paying a little to any one who would teach me the business."

"Got any money?"

"Yes, a little." And I pulled out a handful of change and showed it to him.

"Wal, I'll tell ye what I'll do: I won't be hard on ye, 'cos it'll be some time before ye git any pay. Gimme half a dollar, an' I'll give ye your first lesson right now."

"How about employment?" said I; "will you hire me?"

"I will, me boy; you shall go out with me on my very next trip and continue yer education."

That seemed fair enough, so I handed him the half-dollar.

"Now then let's see ye git up on that car an' set a brake."

I ran lightly up the ladder on the head of the car, and being a vigorous young fellow, gave the brake-wheel what I thought was a good twist up, while he stood on the ground, and stared at me with his mouth open.

I looked down at him to note his approval, but he merely said, "Set it."

"I have," said I.

"Ye have wot?"

"Set the brake."

"W'y, ye hain't took up the slack o' the chain yit. *Set it!*"

He yelled out the words as if I had been half a mile from him instead of twenty feet or so. The sun was now shining down hotly on my back, and the big drops of perspiration ran down from under my straw hat and into my eyes, blinding me.

I could feel my collar, that looked so nice an hour before when I left the hotel, sticking wet and soggy to my neck, as I strained at that old brake-wheel with all my might, blistering my hands with the unfamiliar toil, as I tried vainly, but oh! so hard, to get another notch on it.

With a cry of disgust and derision, the old fellow

came up the ladder like a squirrel, and remarking, "My, but the risin' generation are weakly," he hooked his patent safety coupler, as he called it, on to one of the spokes of the wheel, grasped the rim with his hand, and holding it at arm's length gave his body a swing, when r-r-r-r-uck he spun it round nearly half a turn.

"There!" said he; "that's the way it's done, see? Now kick off the dog an' let 'er go."

I looked at him, and smiled at what I supposed was meant for a pleasantry, but again he roared out, — "Kick off the dog, you d—d fool! W'y don't you kick off the dog?"

I glanced over the car, but there was no dog up there, and I told him so, and furthermore, that I wouldn't kick him off if there was.

With that he grabbed the wheel again, gave it another jerk, and at the same time, with his toe he dexterously kicked the tail of the little ratchet that held it in place; then releasing the wheel, it flew back itself.

"There," said he, pointing with his toe, "that's the dog; now less see ye set it agin."

I had got on to the trick now. So doing as I had seen him, I set it a notch or two tighter than he had, although my hands, unused to the rough iron, were hot and sore. I also by his orders "kicked off the dog an' let 'er go."

"Now," said he, "ye see that simple as it looks, an' strong as ye be, ye couldn't do it till ole Mike showed ye how. Let that teach ye that ye don't know nothin', if ye have been ter school all yer days.

"Now the next thing ye have ter learn is ter jump."

"Jump?" said I.

"Yes, jump. Ye have ter jump off and run inter the telegraph office an' git an order, an' git on agin without the train slowin' up a mite; ye have ter jump off an' run back with a flag, or after the engine's cut loose an' run ahead; ye have ter jump off, an' unlock an' open a switch ter fly in a car that's comin' too durn fast for comfort; an' then agin ye have ter jump ter save yer own bacon, an' that's when ye can't choose neither time nor place, but have got ter git off right where ye be, daylight or dark, on a bridge, on top of a big fill, in a narrow tunnel or deep cut, it don't make no difference, an' the train maybe goin' forty mile an hour. Now I kin git off most anywhere, an' land right side up, so kin Joe there, or at least he could before he got a divorce from his other leg. All of us fellows kin, but I'll bet you're scairt to jump offer this car a stan'nin' right still, down onto that nice smooth ground."

I looked down. It was certainly a high jump, and the ground was tramped down as hard as a barn floor; but I was bound that he shouldn't dare me, and when he added, "I'll never hire a man that can't make a little jump like that, offer a car stan'nin' right still in the yard, for a starter," I stooped for

"It was certainly a high jump." — p. 20.

the spring. A quiet voice from the other side of the car said just then, "What are you doing up there, Mike? Are there any boxes to be packed on the roof of that car?"

I turned and saw a young man of about twenty-five years of age, with a quiet but authoritative manner about him, looking up at us. Mike's important manner dropped from him like a mask, as answering with the one word, "Nothin'," he commenced to descend sullenly to the ground, where the young man waited for him and told him to go on with his work, and quit his tomfoolery, as there was a train of forty cars to go out at four o'clock, or, as he expressed it, at four P.M., and he wanted them all packed before they left.

Looking up at me, he said in the same quiet manner, "Come down here, you," and down I came rather sheepishly, feeling that I had in some way been guilty of something or other, though for the life of me I couldn't imagine what it could be.

"What were you doing up there on that car, detaining this man from his work?" said he, when I arrived on the ground. "Do you know that I could have you locked up for trespassing on the company's property?"

I became greatly alarmed at that, and hastened to assure him that I meant no harm, but that the gentleman who was trimming the switch lamps had directed me to Mr. Mike, who he thought might hire me, as he needed another brakeman, and I was seeking a position of that kind, and that Mr. Mike had been teaching me how to set, and let off a brake, and was just going to teach me jumping when he came up.

I noticed a scarcely perceptible twinkle in his eye as he turned to Mike, who was furiously jabbing dope into an axle-box, and said, —

"Mike, did you intend to hire this young man to brake for you?"

Mike answered never a word; he simply picked up his traps and hurried off to the next car, and I noticed that the lamp-trimmer Joe was also conspicuous by his absence.

"Come with me," said the young man, and when we had gone a little way he asked me if I wished to go braking. I told him I did, and in answer to his further questioning, told him I had never railroaded in any capacity before.

"Very well," said he; "I am the yardmaster here; and as I am rather short of brakemen, and you appear to be a likely young fellow, I will give you a job. But let me advise you to keep away from old Mike and Joe; they were only hoaxing you. Mike is a galvanizer, and has no power to hire anybody. They are two old-time brakemen, who were given those little jobs here in the yard because they were crippled in the company's employ; but they are full of pranks, and delight in playing off their jokes on green hands, so don't take any stock in anything they tell you, and above all, don't take any advice from them, or from any one else, for that matter;

but keep your eyes and ears open; obey orders strictly, *whether you can or not*, and "— here he grabbed me by the arm and pulled me back just as I was about to step directly in front of a rapidly approaching car which an engine had kicked in on that track, and which would certainly have put an end to my railroading there and then.

"— Be careful, never, under any circumstances, no matter how big a hurry you are in, to step upon a railroad track *anywhere*, without first looking both ways; and if you see anything approaching near enough, so that there is any doubt about your being able to cross in perfect safety at an ordinary walk, don't go; always give everything on wheels the right of way."

I have remembered and followed that rule to this day, even in the city streets, and to it I attribute in a great measure the fact that I am alive yet.

"When will you be ready to go to work?" asked the yardmaster. I told him, "Right away." "All right," said he, and then looking at his watch,—

"Well, I don't know but that you had better get your dinner first; it's now eleven thirty, and there's no use of your getting killed on an empty stomach. Do you see that office over there by those green cars?"

"Yes, sir."

"Well, go and get your dinner, and report to me there at 1 P.M. sharp."

"All right, sir," said I, "and thank you very much for your kindness."

"Oh, that's all right; go along now, and be sure and get back on time."

Away I went to my hotel for dinner, highly elated at my success. I was now indeed, I thought, a genuine railroad man. To be sure, I didn't quite like all those allusions to killing and maiming, but I thought they had only been thrown out to try my nerve, and I congratulated myself that I had shown no sign of flinching.

I was wrong in my conjecture, however; for like all railroad yards it was more or less of a slaughterhouse, and one poor fellow's life was crushed out of him that very afternoon, although I didn't hear of it until the next day, and never saw him at all, which was just as well, I guess; for if I had known of it at the time, I dare say I should have lost some of the nerve I felt so proud of.

He was a car-repairer and was at work between two cars on the "dead-head." The car-repairers' signal was a piece of sheet iron, about a foot square, painted blue, and riveted to a four-foot iron rod, sharpened on the bottom so that it could be stuck in a tie vertically.

There was a most rigid order that none but a car-repairer should handle that signal in any manner, and no one but the man that put it up must take it down. All cars needing repairs were run in on this track, and when the men were working on them, they stuck their signal in a tie ahead of the last car put in, and in plain sight of all the men working about the yard.

This was a notice to the train men not to touch any car on that track, or to put any more in there, until the repair gang were notified, so that they might look out for themselves, take down their signal, and put it up again outside the outer car, as before.

In this instance, the signal, carelessly put up, had fallen down, and a conductor having a crippled car to go in there, glanced down the track, saw no signal up, opened the switch, pulled the coupling pin on the crippled car, and gave his engineer a signal to kick it in, which of course he did.

As the unfortunate man was stooping over the drawhead of a car further back, when the kicked car fetched up, the drawhead, link and all, were driven clear through his body.

They said he let one agonizing scream out of him and died. Of course, as soon as they heard him yell, they ran from all directions, but we being in a distant part of the yard knew nothing of it. A switch-rope was hooked on to the car on whose drawhead he was impaled, and the same engine that did the deed pulled it back.

He was a poor man, with the usual poor man's blessing, a large family, so we made up a purse to bury him, and the company gave his wife and two oldest children employment in the car-cleaning gang, and one more was added to the countless thousands of human lives fed into the insatiate maw of the railway.

CHAPTER III.

HE REPORTS FOR DUTY — A RAILROAD MAN AT LAST — BREAKING IN — DIRTY BILL THE ENGINEER — A WALTON PUNKIN HUSKER — THOROUGHLY DISGUSTED — RECEPTION AT THE HOTEL — CONGENIAL COMPANY AT LAST — THE FIRST SQUEEZE

I REPORTED to the yardmaster ten minutes ahead of time. Sticking his head out of the door, he called out, —

"Hey, Simmons!"

A fine, large, sunburned, black-bearded man appeared in answer to the summons.

"Here's a green man I want you to break in," said the yardmaster; "put him on top and let him pass the signal for a day or two until he can handle himself."

"All right," said Simmons, who I soon found was the conductor of a "drill," a switch engine crew. He took me out to the engine, and said to the engineer, a grimy, greasy individual, —

"Bill, here's a fresh fish Dawson wants to break in. I'll put him on the head car and let him pass the signal."

"All right," said Bill, sourly.

I was then told to mount the car next the engine, and repeat the signals of the man in the middle of the train to the engineer.

That seemed simple enough, but I hadn't been doing it more than ten minutes, when the engine stopped, and Bill called out, —

"Hey! Hey! you there, dominie, parson!"

Seeing that he was addressing his remarks to me, and not liking the impertinence of such a disreputable-looking individual, I said, —

"Well! what is it? Are you talking to me?"

"Yes, I'm talkin' to you, an' ye better keep a civil tongue in yer head, I tell ye. What kind of a signal is that ye're givin' me? Wha' d'ye want me ter do, anyway?"

"I don't want you to do anything, and I don't care what you do. I'm giving you the signal just as I get it."

"No, ye hain't nuther, an' don't ye give me no back talk. Say, where do you come from?"

"I am from Walton," said I.

"Sho! I thought so — another Walton punkin husker. Say, Simmons, take this d—d ornament o' yours down off o' here, an' give me a man that knows one signal from another, or I'll smash all the cars in the yard before night."

Then he gave the engine a jerk back that nearly threw me off the car.

"Oh, he's all right," said Simmons. "He's a little green, but he'll get over that;" then to me, "Be careful how you pass the signals, bub, or the engineer can't tell what he's doing."

I told him I was giving them just exactly as the other man did.

"Well, that's all right; Bill is kinder cranky, but you mustn't mind that."

We hadn't worked ten minutes more, and my arms were beginning to ache from the continuous motion, when Bill roared out, —

"Say! you infernal counter-jumper, will you git out o' the way, so I can see that man's signals? Set down, fall down, git ter h— down off o' there! You'll scare the engine off the track, the way you're flapping your wings." Then, having occasion to go to the other end of the yard, he pulled her wide open, drenching me with soot and water from the stack, until I was a sight for gods and men. I had my best clothes on, and they were ruined.

When we were relieved at six o'clock, I was tired, dirty, and thoroughly disgusted with railroading, and started for my hotel firmly determined to quit at once.

Arriving at the door, I found it occupied by the landlord's burly figure, to the exclusion of any one who might wish to pass either in or out. I bid him good evening as cordially as I could, — which wasn't very cordially, — and waited for him to step aside so that I could go in; but without moving, he merely looked down at me, and said in a most insulting tone, —

"Well, what do *you* want?"

I said I wished to go in and get my supper.

"Supper, hey? You'll get no supper here. I don't keep tramps. Come now, get a move on, before I set the dog on you."

"Why, I board here; I arrived last night on the eleven o'clock train from Walton," said I.

"Oh, came in on a brake beam, did you? I thought p'raps you came in your private carriage, — now then, git!"

Seizing me by the shoulders, he whirled me quickly round, and with a vigorous kick, landed me sprawling in a mud puddle in front of the door.

It was my first experience of a kick, and while it was exceedingly painful to my physical person, the insult, which was emphasized by the uproarious laughter of the bystanders, as I rose dripping from the mud, filled me with murderous rage. Rushing upon the piazza, I seized a heavy chair, and raising it over my head went for him; but before I got within range, the dog seized me, — fortunately by the heel of my shoe, — and at the same instant Simmons, who had just arrived, took the chair from me, and driving off the dog, asked what the matter was.

I was now on the point of blubbering outright, but avoided it by an effort of will, while the landlord was bursting with offended dignity, and ordered his clerk to find an officer at once, and have the tramp locked up.

Fortunately for me, however, the clerk recognized

me in spite of my disreputable appearance, and as Simmons explained how I came to be so dishevelled, they managed to pacify the enraged landlord sufficiently to save me from arrest. He notified me, however, that he drew the line at firemen and brakemen; engineers and conductors he would entertain, but no railroaders of lower degree. Thus I took my first lesson in railroad caste, and it was thoroughly impressed on both my mental and physical person.

I swore to sue him for assault and battery; but Simmons dissuaded me, saying he was too big a man for me to successfully prosecute, so I pocketed my injured pride, as I have often had to do since.

My valise was passed out to me, the landlord very graciously declining to charge anything for my previous entertainment, and by Simmons' advice I went to a regular railroad boarding-house, where I soon found the surroundings more congenial, and learned many wise railroad axioms.

During the evening I scraped acquaintance with a young fellow about my own age. I was attracted by his appearance, he seeming to be, like myself, "a boy from home," although not as green as I was. He was a nice, quiet, decent-appearing young fellow who was conspicuous — to me at least — by his non-indulgence in tobacco and profanity.

After supper we adjourned with our chairs to the shade of a big tree in front of the house, and I confided to him my day's woes. He laughed at first; but seeing I regarded my adventures as anything but funny, checked himself, and told me not to mind it; that all green hands were subjected to similar and frequently much worse initiations, and when I told him I would railroad no more, he said I was foolish, he had been at it a year and liked it, and he predicted that inside of thirty days I would too. He said he wouldn't go back to the farm for anything. He sent most of his money home, thereby helping his poor old parents more than he could in any other way.

He admitted that the talk I had heard so much of, in regard to killing and maiming, was by no means exaggerated, but believed that it was largely due to the recklessness of the men themselves, and he hoped to escape the almost universal fate by being careful. Poor fellow! he was blown from the top of his train a few months afterwards, and found by the section gang, frozen stiff.

Being considerably cheered by my new friend's advice, and the good-natured, jolly appearance of other boarders, who seemed pleased to make a new acquaintance, and were quite free with advice and criticisms of everybody above them, from the yard-master to the president of the road, I reconsidered my decision, and reported for duty at six o'clock the next morning, and worked all day with no more thrilling adventure than an occasional cursing from sooty Bill, which, however, I soon learned to disregard entirely.

Before I had been a week in the yard, I was well broken in, and had acquired the reckless air which is the second stage in the greenhorn's experience, and is characteristic of the period *before* he gets hurt.

I delighted in catching and riding on the most swiftly flying cars, and became an expert at making h— fired couplings and flying switches. Occasionally an old hand would say, with a wise shake of the head, "You'll git it bimeby," but I only laughed.

It was four or five months before I "got it." I was making a coupling one afternoon, had balanced the pin in the drawhead of the stationary car, and was running along ahead of the other, holding up the link, when just before coming together she left the track, having jumped a frog. Hearing the racket behind me, I sprang to one side; but my toe touching the top of the rail prevented me from getting quite clear. I was caught between the corners of the cars as they came together and heard my ribs cave in, like smashing an old box with an axe.

The car stopped just right to hold me as in a vice. I nearly fainted with pain, and from inability to breathe. Fortunately Mr. Simmons was watching me, and with the rare presence of mind due to long service he called at once for the switch-rope. He wouldn't allow the engine to come back and couple to the car again, as it would be almost sure to crush out my little remaining life. It seemed to me that I should surely suffocate before they got that switch-rope hooked on to the side of the car, though I knew the boys were hustling for dear life; but I tell you

"I delighted in catching and riding on the most swiftly flying cars." — p. 32.

when your breath is shut off, seconds are hours. My head was bursting, and I became blind; there was a terrible roaring in my ears, and then as the engine settled back on the switch-rope, I felt a life-giving relief as I fell fainting but thankful into the arms of the boys.

I was carried to the yardmaster's office, every step of the way the jagged ends of my broken ribs pricking and grating as though they would punch holes in me, and my breath coming in short suffocating gasps. The company's doctor was summoned, a young fellow fresh from college, whose necessities compelled him to accept the twenty-five dollars a month which they paid for medical attendance for damaged employees. He cut my clothes off, and after half murdering me by punching and squeezing, asking all the time what I was hollering about, finally remarked, —

"There's nothing much the matter with him; few of his slats stove in, that's all." He then bandaged me, and a couple of the boys half carried and half led me to the boarding-house, where I was mighty glad to be, for I was pretty well exhausted.

There I lay unable to move, without help, for six weeks, visited by the doctor daily for a while, and then at less frequent intervals; but some of the boys were with me nearly all the time. They kept me posted as to what was going on in the yard, and cheered me up greatly by telling of their own various mishaps in the past. I found to my surprise that few of them had escaped broken bones and smashed fingers, and I was assured that broken ribs were nothing, absolutely nothing; I ought to have a broken leg or dislocated shoulder pulled into place; then I would know something about it.

Their talk restored my spirits wonderfully; for whereas I had been disconsolate at the thought that I was now a physical wreck, fit only for a job of flagging on some road-crossing at twenty dollars a month, I now found that the boys whom I had seen racing about the yard all day, shouting, giving signals, and climbing on and off cars, had nearly all of them been much worse broken up than I was, and some of them several times, yet they were apparently as sound as ever. Even Simmons, who appeared to be a particularly fine specimen of physical manhood, told me that he once fell while running ahead of a car, just as I had been doing, and twelve cars and the engine passed over him, rolling him over and over, breaking both his legs, and, as he said, mixing up his insides in such a way that his victuals didn't do him much good for a year after.

I was laid up two months, and the very first day I returned to work, I saw a sight that nearly discouraged me altogether. There were two brothers in one of the drill crews: one was conductor, and the other brakeman. As frequently happens, Pete, the conductor, considered his brother Jim the poorest man in the crew, and of course himself the best, so he was always shouting and yelling at him.

On this occasion I was on the ground, giving the signal to Simmons, who passed it on to the engineer, when I heard Pete hollering as usual at Jim, telling him to either pull the pin, or get to h— out o' there and let a *man* do it. There was nothing unusual about that, but I glanced in their direction just in time to see Pete rush at Jim in a rage, yank him out from between the cars, and step in himself.

They were coming back pretty lively, and he wanted to kick the last car in on a spur, and proceed back with the rest of his train without stopping. It had to be done just right, and mighty quick, in order to be a success; that was why he was so aggravated at Jim for not getting the pin out fast enough.

Before he could get the pin out himself, his foot caught in the guard rail, opposite the frog. He grabbed the step of the car, and hung with a death grip for an instant; but it was no use, his foot was tightly wedged. I distinctly saw his face as the step was torn from his grasp, and it haunted me long afterward. A dozen cars went over him before the engine stopped, and his remains were scattered along the track, and ground into small fragments.

I turned sick and faint, and for the rest of that day, every time I thought of his white, agonized face, I was nearly overcome.

CHAPTER IV

RAILROAD MEN'S THEORIES IN REGARD TO MAIMING AND KILLING — A CASE IN POINT — ANOTHER — ON THE ROAD — THE CABOOSE — ON THE ENGINE — TOM RILEY — A CLEVER TRICK

In the boarding-house that evening I expressed my horror at the fate that had befallen poor Pete, and was surprised to find that among the men his was not considered by any means a deplorable case, but if anything rather fortunate; for they argued that he had no time to suffer, and that he was much better off dead than he would have been if crippled for life.

While this argument may seem rather heartless, I must confess that years of experience have since taught me its truth. I have seen and conversed with many men who have survived terrible accidents, and their universal testimony has been that they experienced no suffering at the time, but had simply lapsed into unconsciousness, so that now when I read in the papers the heart-rending details of the horrible deaths by railroad wreck, of those who were *killed*, they fail to move me, for I know that theirs was an enviably easy exit.

I knew a fireman who worked two or three hours

getting his engine ready, backed on to the train, and fired for twenty miles on the road, when, on rounding a curve, the engineer, seeing a locomotive headlight in front of him, shouted to the fireman to jump. Instinctively he pulled the firebox door open, and blinded by the glare of the fire, jumped square out into the darkness.

He was rolled over, and over, and very badly hurt; his face was fearfully cut and lacerated, and several bones were broken.

Both men had seen the headlight through the trees before rounding the curve, but as they got no flag, supposed, of course, that she was on her own track.

It was the way freight that had crossed over to load some freight that had been left on the station platform on that side. The conductor had sent his flag ahead, to hold opposing trains, but the flagman, instead of attending to business, set his red lamp on a tie, and taking the white one, went looking for chestnuts in the woods. The red lamp, left to itself, went out, and hence the collision.

When the engineer saw that it was inevitable, he shut off, reversed, and blew brakes. She was one of those old-fashioned engines, with the throttle stem through the boiler head; so that when he had done all in his power to stop, and it was too late to jump, the tender at the moment of collision leaped up and pinned the unfortunate man fast to the hot boiler head. The coal shooting forward, from the sudden stoppage, filled the cab, and buried him completely from sight.

When the train men came to look for the engine crew, they were nowhere to be found, but soon the odor of roasting human flesh gave them the clew, and procuring shovels they frantically threw out the coal, only to find the dead engineer sole occupant of the wreck. Knowing that the fireman had either jumped or been thrown off, one party searched the track with lanterns, and soon found him in the ditch covered with blood and dirt, his clothes nearly all torn off, and apparently dead.

He revived, however, after being carried into the station, and the application of such simple but effective remedies as railroad men know of. He appeared to have entirely recovered his senses, told what he knew of the wreck, and expressed genuine sorrow for the fate of his engineer. A passenger train was flagged, and he was sent into the hospital; he conversed as well as he could with the train crew, telling them all that had happened, not only what he knew himself, but also what the others had told him. After his wounds were dressed in the hospital, he was taken with a fever, and for several days hovered between life and death.

On his recovery he was unable to remember a single circumstance later than the eating of his dinner at home on the day of the wreck.

I knew an engineer who had occasion to jump, and not liking the looks of the big rock fill on his side, he jumped down in the tender where the fireman was watching for a good chance on his own side. They were both picked up for dead, but whether they jumped or were thrown off neither could ever tell: the last thing the engineer remembered was telling the fireman to hurry up, so that he could get off too.

Shortly after my return to work Simmons got one side of a new freight train, and to my great delight took me with him on the road. I was not only glad to get out of the slaughter-house, with my full complement of limbs, but I was also pleased at the prospect of at last learning practical railroading, of which I had heard so much.

We had a fine big eight-wheel caboose, right out of the paint shop, red outside, and green inside. There were six bunks in her, a row of lockers on each side, to sit on and keep supplies in, a stove and table, and a desk for the conductor. We furnished our own bedding and cooking-utensils, and as Simmons wouldn't have any but nice fellows around him, we had a pleasant and comfortable home on wheels. We each contributed to the mess, except the flagman, and as he did the cooking, he messed free. We took turns cleaning up, and as the boys had good taste, we soon had the car looking like a young lady's boudoir. We had lace curtains in front of the bunks, a strip of oil cloth on the floor, a mat that the flagman had "swiped" from a sleeper, a canary in a cage, and a dog.

As a younger man than I had been assigned to us, I was second man, which gave me the head of the train; so I rode on the engine, and was the engineer's flag.

I ran ahead when necessary to protect our end, opened and closed switches, cut off and coupled on the engine, held the train on down grades, watched out for the caboose on curves, took water, shovelled down coal to the fireman, rang the bell at crossings, put on the blower, oiled the valves, and handed the engineer oil-cans, wrenches, and lights for his pipe.

I now scraped acquaintance with that formidable document, the time table, and heard train orders, and the officers who issued them, discussed by such high authorities as conductors and engineers, and I listened in rapt astonishment at the deep erudition which they displayed in handling these subjects. I soon learned that the officers on our road "didn't know nothing," and that "where *I* come from" they would not have been allowed to "sit on the fence and watch the trains go by," whereupon I conceived a great wonder as to how the road survived under such densely incompetent management.

I enjoyed riding on the engines, as the engineers and firemen were fine, sociable fellows, and when we were a little late, and had a passing point to make, the engineer would sometimes say, "Don't you set no brakes goin' down here; I got to git a gait on 'em." Then when the train pitched over the top of the hill, he would cut her back a notch at a time, till

"I watch that grimy left hand on the throttle." — p. 41.

he got her near the centre, and gradually work his throttle out wide open. How she would fly down hill, the exhaust a steady roar out of the stack, the connecting-rods an undistinguishable blur, the old girl herself rolling and jumping as if at every revolution she must leave the track, the train behind half hid in a cloud of dust, and I hanging on to the side of the cab for dear life, watching out ahead where I know there is a sharp reverse curve, and hoping, oh, so much, that he'll shut her off before we get there.

I watch that grimy left hand on the throttle for the preliminary swelling of the muscles, that will show me he is taking a grip on it to shove it in. Not a sign; his head and half his body are out the window; and now we are upon it. I give one frightened glance at the too convenient ditch, where I surely expect to land, and take a death grip of the side of the cab. Whang! She hits the curve, seems to upset; I am nearly flung out the window in spite of my good grip. Before she has half done rolling (how do the springs ever stand it?) she hits the reverse, and I am torn from my hold on the window and slammed over against the boiler, and having passed this most uncomfortable place, she flies on, rolling and roaring down the mountain. All this time the engineer hasn't moved an eyelid, nor the firemen interrupted for an instant the steady pendulum-like swing of the fire-door and the scoop-shovel. How do they do it? Oh, it's easy after you get used to it.

Fifteen minutes afterward, in the siding, with switches locked waiting for the flyer, nobody seems to remember that we have done anything in particular.

At first I had considered the locomotive as far too complicated a machine for me ever to understand, but gradually I learned its various parts; and when I found that nearly all the engineers and firemen had risen from brakemen like myself, I took heart, and hoped that some day I might sit on the right side, to be spoken to with some slight deference by the officials, and stared at in open-mouthed admiration by the small boys at the country stations.

Old Tom Riley was a man to whom I looked up as the epitome of railroad knowledge. He frequently hauled our train; he was so old that the top of his head was perfectly bald, but he had a great mop of gray beard, with a yellowish streak from the chin down, an evidence of many years of tobacco-chewing, and unsuccessful efforts to spit to windward.

He was supposed to be the oldest engineer anywhere about, and said himself, that his "first job railroadin' wos wipin' the donkey engine in Noah's ark." He was a good-natured, jolly old fellow, a great practical joker, strong, and rough as a bear, but as well pleased apparently when the joke was on himself, as any other way. He had been so long at the business that he knew all sorts of tricks by which to get himself out of tight places, so that it was seldom indeed that the "super" had the pleasure of hauling Tom on the carpet for a violation of the rules.

One night we were a little late, so that we barely had time to make the siding for a following passenger train, and to make matters worse, when we were about halfway there, Tom said he smelt something hot, so he stopped, and found his main crank-pin about ready to blaze up. The oil-cup had stopped feeding; so he deliberately took it out, filled the hole with tallow, screwed in the cup, called his flag, and started again, very late.

Simmons came up over the train and said he guessed he'd leave a flag at the bottom of the hill to hold No. 6 till we got in.

"No, no," says old Tom; "don't ye never drop off no flag to give yourself away, git called ter the office, an' all hands git ten days."

"You can't get to the switch on time," said Simmons.

"Course not. I ought ter be there in twenty minutes, an' I'll be lucky if I git there in twenty-five."

"Well, then, I'll have to drop off a flag, or they'll git our 'doghouse.'"

"Now here, Simmons, I'll tell ye what you do: you go back in the doghouse, an' don't you see nothin' that's goin' on; only git up in the cupalo an' watch out good an' sharp that yer train don't break in two. I'll git ye inter the switch time enough, so six'll never see yer tail lights."

Simmons, knowing his man, at last agreed, and

after he had got safely housed, Tom handed me his long oil-can, and told me to go back on the step of the caboose, and oil first one rail, and then the other.

"Let the oil run about a car length on one rail, an' then do the same the other side; repeat the dose once, an' come ahead agin," said Tom.

I did so, and just as we were pulling in to the side track, we heard the exhaust of the passenger engine, as she came clipping along for the hill; presently we could tell by the sound that she had struck the grade, then — cha-cha-ch-r-r-r cha-ch-r-r-r.

"Oho!" says Tom, "are ye there? Grind away, my boy. I guess old Tom 'll git in an' git the switch locked before you git up here, all right."

He did, too. Long before the passenger engine got by the oil, we were comfortably smoking our pipes in the switch, and when she went sailing by, her engineer shouted something that we couldn't catch, but to which Tom replied, —

"Go ahead, sonny; you're all right."

Next day, as Tom was doing a little packing in the roundhouse, the engineer of "six" came up to him and said, —

"Riley, was that you in Snyders' when I went by last night?"

"Yes," says Tom. "A little late, wa'n't ye?"

"Late? I sh'd say so. I never saw Snyders' so slippery as 'twas last night. I used half a box of sand. How'd you git there?"

"Oh, I didn't have no trouble," says Tom. "I

"Her engineer shouted something that we couldn't catch." — p. 44.

didn't notice that 'twas any slipperyer 'n usual; guess maybe the pet cock on yer pump might 'a' been leakin' a little or suthin, an' wet the rail fer ye."

"Mebbe so," says the other fellow; and away he went to look his engine over, and see if such was the case.

CHAPTER V

APPLIES FOR A FIREMAN'S POSITION — KEEPING HER TAIL UP — A MISTAKE IN ORDER — A BAD WRECK — A HAIR-BREADTH ESCAPE

I "BROKE" a year, and by that time was of some use. I could read the time table, discuss train orders, and knew the trains by heart. I had written to my mother, telling her that I was employed on the railroad, but not in what capacity. I heard in reply that my father was far from well, and while the news damped my spirits momentarily, I soon forgot it, in the excitement of things of more immediate interest to myself.

I came to the conclusion that the engine offered more opportunities of advancement than the caboose, so by Tom Riley's advice I filed an application with the master mechanic, asking for a position as fireman; and though I must admit that he didn't give me the slightest encouragement, yet the fact that I had my application on file made me feel that I was sure of a job, and that, too, at no very distant day, so I began to take a greater interest than ever in the engines, and I presume I made a nuisance of myself by asking innumerable questions of the engineers and firemen, so anxious was I to learn all I could in regard to the machine, for which, even to this day, I have an abiding love and respect. The amount of misinformation that I acquired was sufficient to have wrecked any road in the country, if I had been in a position to put it into effect. Some, no doubt, was given me unconsciously, or rather mischievously, that I might make a show of myself in the arguments in which I was so fond of indulging with the firemen; but by far the larger part due to the ignorance of those on whom I relied for information, for at this period I was unable to distinguish between those who were and those who were not competent to furnish what I was so desirous of obtaining. To me it seemed that all alike, engineers and firemen, were good authorities on the subject, though before I got through with them I was pretty well able to sift the wheat from the chaff.

Sometimes when the train was not too heavy, and the grade was favorable, one or other of the firemen would let me "take her" for a bit; and then if I was able to "keep her tail up," I felt myself indeed a man, and never failed to let it be known in the caboose that I had fired on a certain stretch of the road. But if while I was at the shovel she dropped her tail, and the fireman had to take her from me, I would not allude to that episode, when bragging of my abilities; but the men were sure to hear of it, and the guying I got fully offset my petty triumphs.

About six months after I filed my application, there was a mistake made in orders, that came very near winding up my railroad career for good. I did not know at the time exactly what the trouble was, nor can I say now positively. Simmons and the engineer, who were both discharged, asserted that they were sacrificed to save the despatcher, who was a son-in-law of the president of the road.

Whoever was to blame, the result was disastrous; for we met the train which we expected to pass at the next siding, in a deep cut under a railroad bridge. Both trains were wheeling down under the bridge at a forty-mile gait, so as to have a good headway on, to take them out the other side. As the view of both engineers was obstructed by the stone abutments of the bridge, neither doubted for a moment that he had a clear track.

They met exactly under the bridge with a shock and roar that seemed to shake the solid earth; the locomotives reared up like horses, the cars shoved their tenders under them in such a way as to jack them up and raise the bridge off its abutments; and then as the cars climbed on top of each other, they battered it from its position until it lay nearly at right angles to its own road like an open draw, resting on top of the wreck.

Our conductors sent flags back both ways to hold all trains; but before the men could get up the bank to flag on the cross-country road, a belated gravel train came hurrying along, and plumped in on top of us, helping to fill up the cut still more. Their engine set fire to the wreck, and as we were some distance

"They met exactly under the bridge." — p. 48.

from a telegraph office, all three trains and engines were entirely consumed before help reached us, nothing remaining but a tangled and twisted mass of boilers, wheels, rods, and pipes, partly covered by the gravel train's load of sand.

I was on the engine, sitting on the fireman's seat, looking out ahead. As it was daylight, there was not even the glare of a head-lamp to give us the fraction of a second's warning, and our own engine made such a roaring in the narrow cut that we could hear nothing else. The first intimation we had of approaching danger was when we saw the front end of the other locomotive not forty feet from us. Neither of the engineers had time to close their throttles — an act that is done instinctively on the first appearance of danger.

I cannot say that I was frightened. Even the familiar "jumping of the heart into the throat," which so well describes the sensation usually experienced on the sudden discovery of deadly peril, was absent; for though I certainly saw the front end of that engine as plainly as I ever saw anything in my life, I had no time to realize what it meant. I made no move or effort of any kind, and it seemed that at the same instant that she burst upon my view, daylight was shut out and I was drenched with cold water; yet before that happened, they had come together, reared up as I have said, and I had been thrown to the front of the cab, the tender had come ahead, staving the cab to pieces, thereby dropping me out on the ground, and by knocking a hole in itself against the back driving-wheel, had deluged me with its contents.

The flood of cold water caused me, bewildered as I was, to try and get away from it. I knew I was under the wreck, and for a few minutes I could hear the cars piling up, and grinding overhead.

I knew what that was too, and feared they would smash the wreck down on top of me, and so squeeze my life out. But the engine acted as a fender; for being jammed among the wreckage, she could not be pushed over, and as she stood on her rear wheels she could not be mashed down.

The noise soon ceased, and then except for the sound of steam escaping from the boilers, I could hear nothing; then I remembered that the boilers themselves were a fruitful source of danger to me, as there might be a hole knocked in the water-space that would pour out a scalding flood and boil me alive. I had heard, too, of boilers in inaccessible localities losing the water from about the furnaces, and getting the iron so hot and soft, that it would give out like wet paper, blowing up and scalding any unfortunate who might be imprisoned near it. I knew, too, that wrecks had a way of taking fire from the locomotive. These thoughts occurred to me much more rapidly than I could tell them, and spurred me on to do my utmost to get out of there.

It was perfectly dark where I was; and, as I knew, it was still daylight outside. This proved to me how completely I was buried under the wreck, and was far from reassuring. How could I ever hope to make my way from under those tons of cars and engines? The only wonder was that I had escaped being killed instantly, and for a few minutes I felt but little gratitude at having been spared, only to be slowly tortured to death.

When I attempted to move, I found that as far as sensation was concerned, my right leg ended at the knee, so I felt down to see if it was cut off, as I knew it would be necessary to stanch the flow of blood in that case, or I would soon die from that cause alone. To my great joy, I found that my leg and foot were still with me, though how badly hurt I was unable to tell, for being drenched with water, the blood might, for all I knew, be flowing from many severe wounds.

At this moment there was another crash, and grinding and splintering overhead, caused by the wrecking of the gravel train, but which I attributed to the explosion of one of the boilers. In this second wreck, two men were killed outright, and the engineer died of his injuries the next day; yet to it, I have no doubt, I owe my escape, for it disturbed the position of the cars, so that I perceived a ray of daylight, away, as it seemed, half a mile ahead of me. I exerted myself to the utmost to reach it, and how far off it was! I had to work my way back under the wrecked tender and several cars. I found the space under the tender piled so full of coal that it was impossible to pass, yet that was my only way out; so I began digging with my hands, feverishly, madly, in the desire to get away while I still had my senses and strength, and oh how I wished then I had never gone railroading! What was there in it? A miserable living gained by the hardest kind of work, with almost a certainty of being crippled, or meeting death by some horrible means.

After digging as it seemed for hours, until my hands were raw and bleeding, and I had blocked my retreat by the coal I had thrown behind me, I found myself confronted by the axle of the rear truck, which stood at such an angle as to positively forbid all hope of my ever getting out that way.

I sank down in despair, realizing that like thousands of poor railroaders who had gone before, my time had now come, and here in this dark close hole was to be the end of me. I tried to fix my mind on such thoughts as I knew were appropriate to the occasion, but my leg was so painful that I could think of nothing else. It seemed to have swollen to twice its size, and I remember thinking as I lay there in what I believed to be my living grave, that I might at least have been spared that extra torment.

A numbness came over me, and I seemed to be falling into a kind of stupor, broken frequently by the twinges of pain from my leg, when my nostrils were greeted by a faint odor of wood smoke, and my heart was thrilled with a new terror that urged me to make one more desperate effort to escape.

"It wasn't long before I crawled under the truck." — p. 53.

The wreck was on fire, and though I might have resigned myself to lie still and die, I could not endure the thought of being roasted alive; so again made desperate by great fear, I dug my bleeding hands into the coal, and commenced to burrow like a woodchuck in the direction where I could see that the truck was elevated highest above the rail, and to my great joy I soon found that the coal pile extended but a short distance in that direction.

It wasn't long before I had crawled under the truck, which had been raised from the ground by the corner of a car, and was making fairly good progress among the tangle of wheels, axles, and brake-gear, in the direction of the ray of light which had first attracted my attention. I found it came down by a very small, crooked, and much-obstructed passage through the débris of broken cars above my head—a passage entirely too small for me to get through, and which I could never hope to enlarge myself. The smoke was now suffocating, and it was only at longer and longer intervals that I could catch my breath. I had not as yet felt the heat of the fire, but when I looked up through the narrow opening above me, I could see in the flying clouds of smoke sparks and small firebrands, which told me that the fire must be raging fiercely, and also that the wind was blowing it in my direction, which induced me to make the most frantic efforts to escape. I might as well have tried to lift the ponderous locomotive, as to move the tightly wedged wreckage that imprisoned me; and as I glanced at the little patch of blue sky, now nearly blotted out in black smoke, an agonizing sense of my desperate situation filled my mind.

Why should I endeavor to keep life in myself until the very last second, only to endure all the suffering there was to be got out of the situation? Why not seek some swift and easy method of escape from the inevitable torture staring me in the face? I opened my pocket knife — it wasn't very sharp, but still it might serve me at a pinch; how much better to open an artery and quietly pass away, than to be suffocated by smoke, or roasted by fire! I sat thinking these desperate thoughts, and waiting, I presume, until my position should become absolutely unbearable, when I saw a man step across my little glimpse of light. Having fortunately just refreshed myself by a breath of fresh air, I let a desperate yell out of me, and saw him stop and look all around, as though saying to himself, "What was that?" "Here! here!" I shouted; "right down in this hole, under your feet!" He looked down, and I recognized him as a brakeman by the name of Ben Shaw, belonging to the other train. "Is there anybody down there?" he asked. "Yes," said I; "and for God's sake hurry up; get men and axes and cut me out; I am nearly smothered, and can't stand it much longer."

"All right," said he; "I'll see what we can do; but I don't believe we can get you out, for the fire is coming this way awful fast."

With this extremely unwelcome assurance he disappeared, but I could hear him shouting as he went, and soon — though it seemed long enough to me — he returned with others, armed with fence-stakes, and wrecking-axes, and they fell to with a will, prying and chopping at the obstruction. On account of the smoke and heat, which was now almost unbearable down where I lay, they were unable to work more than three or four minutes, when they would be driven away, gasping for breath, so that not one blow out of three was effective. A chance blow with an axe loosened a large section of the side of a car, which fell over, one corner striking me a severe blow on the head, cutting the scalp, and nearly knocking me senseless. While apparently opening the way, in reality it closed it, for it fell in such a manner that if I had been above it, I could easily have got out, but now I was completely covered in. It contained the door of the car, however, which was open a few inches, and if I could only pry that door back a little more, I should be able to get through. The question of life or death to me now was, could I do that?

I heard Simmons' voice, interrupted by violent coughing and sneezing, say, "How's that? Can you get out now?" "No," said I; "you'll have to come down in the hole and clear away the door."

"Can't do it; we can't stay here another minute, but I'll throw you down these stakes, and maybe you can help yourself. Good-bye, old man; I'm awful sorry for you." Then there was a clattering that told me he had thrown down the stakes as he said he would.

My eyes were so blinded by the pungent wood smoke, and I was so nearly suffocated, that I had but little strength left. One of the stakes lay right across the slight opening in the door, and in trying to turn it to pull it through, I found I didn't need it, as the door moved freely in its grooves.

I quickly pushed the door back and by a great effort of will and my slight remaining strength dragged myself through the aperture. I wasn't out yet though, for overhead there was a solid sheet of flame roaring in the wind like a furnace, and completely covering my exit. Although still drenched with water, I could feel my hair curling with the intense heat.

There was one course, and one only open to me; so taking as long a breath as I could, I shut my eyes and made a dive for liberty. I scrambled upward, and outward, now burning my hands by contact with hot iron, and again tearing them on the jagged ends of broken wood, my head fairly bursting with the heat and suppressed respiration. Suddenly I stepped forward upon nothing; having no hold with my hands I fell, struck on my side, rebounded and fell again, down, down, I could have sworn for miles — and then unconsciousness came over me.

It seems that when I got out of the hole, I rushed blindly off the end of a blazing car, piled high in the wreck, and in falling I struck on various projections of the wreckage, tearing off nearly all my clothing, which was a providence, as I was all ablaze, and finally brought up with a dull thud, as the reporters say, on solid ground, shaking and bruising myself dreadfully, but almost miraculously breaking no bones, though I had fallen from a height of thirty feet.

My leg which had hindered me so much was merely bruised and crushed, but was as black as your hat for a long time, and I was as bald as the day I was born.

As a crowd of natives had already collected, my somewhat theatrical appearance was not without spectators. It was assumed that I was dead, but kind hands extinguished the fire in my few remaining rags, and it was not long before signs of life were discovered in the bruised and blackened object.

I was carried to a near-by farmhouse and kindly cared for until the wrecking-train returned to town, when I was sent to hospital.

Our engineer escaped without a scratch, but how he never knew; for all he could remember was, that he was looking right at the number plate of the approaching engine, and *at the same time* falling heels over head *up* the side of the cut. Of our fireman not a trace was ever found, and as I heard nothing of him while under the wreck, I have no doubt that he was instantly killed and his body burnt up.

On the other engine, the whole crew, engineer,

fireman, and head brakeman perished, and were consumed in the fierce flames that devoured the wreck and made a blast furnace of the narrow cut. We could only hope that they had been mercifully killed at once, and not slowly roasted alive, as so many have been, and will continue to be while railroads exist.

CHAPTER VI

INVESTIGATION OF THE WRECK — VICTIMIZED BY THE COMPANY — TRAINMEN INDICTED — ACQUITTED — DISAPPOINTMENT — TOM RILEY'S SAGE ADVICE — A RAILROAD AUTOCRAT — DISCHARGED — CHICAGO — FIRING

I REMAINED in hospital about a week; during which time both the coroner and the company's lawyer took my affidavit, as to what I knew of the orders by which we were running. I knew nothing about them, but I observed that the company's attorney appeared anxious to have me remember having heard that we were to meet and pass train 31 at Brookdale, and appeared very much disappointed when I was unable to do so.

Brookdale was the last switch that we passed before the collision. It was claimed by the company, and admitted by the conductor of train 31, that their orders read "meet and pass train 28 at Brookdale." Our orders should have stated the same passing-point, and the company's witnesses all swore they did; they even produced the operator's copy with Simmons' signature attached, in proof. Simmons swore the signature was forged, but as it corresponded with others which they produced on former orders, this statement had but little effect.

Both Simmons and the engineer swore that their orders read "Daly's"; the flagman stated that Simmons invariably read the orders to him, asked him how he understood them, explained them if necessary, and then filed them on a hook in the caboose, where they remained open to inspection until fulfilled, when he put them in his desk, to be returned to the train-despatcher at the end of the trip; he also swore that our order read "Daly's."

The engineer said he always read his copy of all orders to the conductor, to be sure they understood them alike; he then filed them on a hook in the cab, and when the hook was full, threw them in the firebox.

Asked by the company's attorney if he made a practice of reading his orders to the fireman and head brakeman, he said no; but if they asked what the orders were, he told them, and gave them any information they asked for. For this neglect to read orders to every man within reach he was severely censured by both the lawyer and the coroner, although there was no rule requiring him to do so; "For," said the lawyer, "if you had done so, probably some of those men might not have been quite so pigheaded as you are, and would have remembered that Brookdale was your meeting-point."

The engineer replied that he now wished he had, as in that case he would have had at least one witness (me) to prove that the despatcher was to blame for the wreck.

As the conductor's and the engineer's copies had been destroyed in the fire, and as the majority of the evidence was against them, the coroner's jury censured them for the wreck, and they were indicted by the grand jury for manslaughter.

During the time that elapsed between the indictment and the trial, the operator who received the order, and swore that it read "Brookdale," was transferred from his little station in the woods to the best paying station on the road, and the conductor of train 31 was promoted over the heads of half a dozen older men, to a first-class passenger train. By these apparent acts of bribery, public opinion became so biassed against the company, that the defendants' lawyer easily procured an acquittal, which threw the responsibility upon the company, and the suits for damages which ensued, with their rapidly accumulating costs, finally bankrupted it.

About a week after I left the hospital, as I felt able to return to work, I resolved to apply again for a fireman's position, knowing that a vacancy existed, owing to the death of the man on train 31. I called on the master mechanic, whom I found alone in his office, and asked respectfully if he would give me the vacant place, reminding him that my application had been on file for some time.

He was writing, and without even looking up answered "No," and that was all I could get out of him, though I tried to find out why he wouldn't appoint me, and when I might expect him to do so. Feeling deeply disappointed, and not a little hurt at the manner of my reception, I walked out, and strolled over to the round-house, to have a look at the engines which had all at once become so unattainable to me.

I had taken a great interest in the engines. It was a promotion, a step higher, to which I had looked forward with great eagerness, and now to have all my hopes dashed at once, and for no cause that I could see, was very discouraging.

I espied Tom Riley at work on his engine and stated my case to him, asking what I could do now that the master mechanic had dashed my hopes. I told him how anxious I was to get on the left side of the locomotive, and begged the veteran for advice. He listened to my tale of woe patiently, and appeared interested. When I finished, he said:—

"I'll tell you where you made the mistake, boy."

"Where?" said I, anxiously.

"In goin' to that long, starved-to-death, white-livered hound of a master mechanic, an' askin' him for anything. Don't ye know there's only one thing he delights in more 'n another, an' that is hearin' that a man wasn't killed in a wreck, so he can discharge him when he gits back? I tell you, boy, you have done the only thing you could do to please him to-day, an' that is, you gave him a chance to refuse you somethin'; but 'tain't you he's pleased with, its himself; so his pleasure won't do you no good, an' don't you delude yerself with the idee that 'twill. Do you know what he's doin' now? Wal, I'll tell you; he's got two vacancies to fill: one is that of the fireman who was killed, an' the other the engineer who was discharged for not gittin' killed; an' now he's puzzlin' his brains to find somebody that don't want either of them jobs, but that is in his power, so he can make 'em take 'em agin their will. If you had gone into his office this mornin' rippin' an' ravin', an' said, 'See here, I've heard that you was agoin' to appoint me to the vacancy caused by the death of Pete Russell, an' I've come in to let you know, that I don't want it, an' won't have it under no consideration, an' I wouldn't work in your department for ten dollars a day.' If you'd talked to him like that, he would have appointed you, an' made you take it too; but now of course it's too late. The trouble with you young fellers is, that you've got so much infernal conceit, you think you know it all, so you won't ask the advice of an old fool till you git stuck; then after you've made a complete mess of the whole business, *then* you come a whinin' an' a cryin' round, an' it's, 'Oh, Tom, what shall I do now?' Well, I'll tell you, the only thing you can do now is to go to the super; tell him jest how the case stands, an' mebbe he'll make the master mechanic app'int ye, an' prob'ly he won't; anyhow, that's your only chance. An' say, ye can tell him that ye are recommended by Mr. Thomas Riley, Engineer, if ye like."

"All right," said I, and thanking the old man for his advice, I went at once to the superintendent's office, not, however, with any very great confidence in the success of my errand; for I had been long enough at the business now to know that there was such a thing as official courtesy on railroads, and I doubted that the superintendent would order the master mechanic to appoint me against his will.

I was bound, however, to see the thing through, so I walked boldly into the office, and inquired for the superintendent. I learned that he was in, and sat down to wait the gentleman's pleasure. A good long wait I had of it, too; several times he came into the room where I was, but he was evidently very busy, and paid no attention to me. Presently he came rushing out with his hat on, pulling on his coat as he went, and his exit seemed to be the signal for dinner; for all the clerks bolted immediately in his rear, leaving me the sole occupant of the office. I, too, went home, bolted my dinner in a hurry, and hastened back, fearing to miss him on his return; for it is an old saying on the railroad, that the best time to catch a boss is on his return from lunch, when he is supposed to be in a good humor, and more apt to receive a petition favorably than at any other time. I found I was successful so far as that he had not returned before me.

I sat and squirmed in discomfort on that hard bench until after three o'clock; then he came bustling in, and as usual passed me by. Tired with my long wait, I tiptoed to the chief clerk's desk and asked in a whisper if he thought Mr. Wilkes would see me now. "What do you want with him?" said he. I told him I was seeking a fireman's position on the road. As he didn't appear to have anything else to do, he amused himself by pumping the whole story out of me, and then coolly told me he didn't think the super would see me that day, as he was very busy. I had better call some other time. His offhand way of disposing of what was a very important matter to me, roused my ire to such an extent that I declined to act on his suggestion, but, on the contrary, I promised myself that I would see and speak to that super, even if I had to force my way into his sanctum.

It was nearly five o'clock when he appeared, bound, as I felt sure, for home. "Now or never," said I, and I stepped up to the gentleman, asking for a few minutes of his valuable time. He stopped short, whirled half-round, pulled out an old-fashioned silver watch with a jerk, looked at it abstractedly, for a moment, and then asked brusquely, "Well, what is it? Talk quick now; I'm in a hurry." I stated my case as briefly as possible. "Well, what do you want me to do?" said he.

I told him that Mr. Tom Riley, an engineer, had advised me to see him, thinking, perhaps, he might intercede with the master mechanic in my behalf.

"Ever railroad any?"

"Yes, sir; nearly two years on this road."

"What doing?"

"Braking, sir."

"When did you quit?"

"I haven't quit at all; I was braking for Simmons at the time of the wreck, and have just come from the hospital."

His face flushed angrily, as he replied, "The h— you were! Well, I admire your gall!" Turning to the head clerk, he added, "Mr. Clark, have this fellow's time made out, and hand it to him," and he was off.

"Have this fellow's time made out." That meant that I was discharged, and in Heaven's name, for what? I was not conscious of having done anything to merit such harsh treatment, and the sudden verdict, from which I knew there was no appeal, nearly floored me. It was a new experience, and as unexpected as it was unwelcome. It was some time before I was able to obtain any information explaining the super's conduct; at last, however, a brakeman told me that I had been discharged ever since the wreck, only, having been in hospital, I had not heard of it.

"So," said he, "when you told him you was still on the road, he thought you had come up to the office to have a little fun with him, and it made him mad."

Have fun with the superintendent? Not I. I had not yet reached the reckless stage of the hardened veteran who smokes his pipe in the powder magazine.

I asked the braky why I should be discharged, as I had no hand in causing the wreck. "You refused to swear that the meet and pass order read Brookdale, didn't you?"

"Certainly; how could I swear when I didn't know anything about it?"

"Well, that's your misfortune, my boy; if you can't swear to what the company wants, just because you don't know, you must expect to suffer for your lack of ability," saying which, he left me with the air of a superior being who had kindly shed some of his superabundant light on my benighted ignorance.

After the first shock of bitter disappointment I took a philosophical view of the situation. It was not, after all, such a dreadful thing to be discharged. I remembered how I had heard the men frequently, in relating their experiences, laugh heartily at old So-and-so, who had fired them for accidents, or infraction of rules, as though it was a joke. I could now travel, see how work was done on other roads, and with the swagger of an old hand make use of the time-honored phrase, "where I come from," that somewhat hazy and indefinite locality where everything is perfect, in glittering contrast with "this road," which is "the worst I ever saw."

At twelve o'clock that night I boarded a Chicago-bound freight train, for I was determined hereafter to railroad only from the great centre itself. The crew of the train, who were all my friends, made me comfortable in the caboose, expressed themselves as sorry to see me going, but advised me to keep a stiff upper lip, saying that I would have no trouble getting a job in Chicago, where experienced railroad men were always in demand; for at that time the country was not overrun with them, as it is now. I was passed along from one road to another, my transportation costing me nothing, until one morning bright and early I landed in Chicago, with a little money in my pocket, my heart as light as a feather, strong, confident, and fearless, and I set out in search of that which so many are always seeking — a job. I determined to brake no more. I would only try for a fireman's position, and to my inexperience it seemed that I would only have to let it be generally known that I was ready to go to work, to have all the trunk lines contending for my valuable services. Undue self-appreciation is, however, easily corrected. Before looking for employment I did what every countryman always does, — took in the sights; and as I remember them they were not very wonderful, therefore they filled my uncultivated mind with wonder.

This mild dissipation encroached on my treasury to such an extent as to remind me that my visit to the metropolis was one of business, and not pleasure; so after a couple of days' sight-seeing, I started out in earnest to find employment.

My first day's catch amounted only to a fine assortment of refusals, the second was a repetition of the first, and I began to realize that Chicago would have survived some time without my presence within her borders.

On the third day as I was strolling rather listlessly

through a certain round-house, I overheard a conversation between the foreman and caller, which told me that there was a fireman wanted in a hurry. As I was now at that stage in the game where any job was a good job, I stepped up to the man and asked if he was the round-house foreman. He said he was.

"I'm looking for a job, sir," said I.

"Can you fire?"

"Yes, sir."

"Where have you fired?"

"On the —— road."

"All right; go over to the master mechanic's office and ask for Mr. Seely, tell him Phelps sent you, and if he hires you, come right back to me. I want you to go out on that engine right away. Hurry up, now!"

"All right, sir," said I, and away I went on the run, stealing a hasty glance, as I went, at the engine standing at the water-plug. As I remember her now, she was a common enough old trap; but I thought then that she was a masterpiece, and mentally prayed that I might be hired, and appointed to preside over the scoop and tallow-pot of that magnificent roadster.

My business with the head of the mechanical department was briefly and satisfactorily settled, and he told me to report to Phelps at once.

Phelps told me to "git right on to 227; there's the oil-room," pointing to a low, dingy structure. "Hurry up now; git yer supplies, an' git out o' here!" So I was hired.

CHAPTER VII

HE CATCHES A TARTAR — ALL PREVIOUS RECORDS BROKEN — JOSEPH H. GRINNELL, THE OMNIPOTENT ENGINEER — DEFIANCE — HE MAKES FRIENDS — HAULED UPON THE CARPET — DISCHARGED AGAIN — FRIENDS IN NEED — PHELPS IS PLEASED — HE "WIPES" FOR FIFTEEN MONTHS — SQUARES ACCOUNTS WITH JOSEPH H. GRINNELL

As I stepped up on the tender and opened the oil-box to get the cans, the most disagreeable-looking face that I ever saw presented itself at the opposite gangway, and a thin, squeaky voice called out: —

"Hey! what are ye up to? What ye doin' there?"

I asked him if he was the engineer.

"Who d'ye s'pose I be, ye blamed fool? The president of the road?"

"No," said I; "I thought you was the board of directors."

"The h—ll you did! Well, now you git down out o' there, and direct yourself somewheres else."

"Say, Pap," said I, " I don't know nor care a continental who you are; but I'm going to fire this engine to-night, and if you don't like it, now's your time to kick."

That made him mad. He shoved his oil-can and

wrench up into the tender, and away he went across the yard shouting, "Hey, Phelps!" But Phelps kept out of his way. When I got back from the oil-room, he was in the cab waiting for me, and the instant I set the cans upon the foot-board, he rang the bell and gave her a vicious jerk back; but I had climbed too many flying freight cars to be disturbed by that. I swung myself lightly aboard, and gave him a black look, which didn't mend matters any; for I was satisfied that he was a crank, and that it would be poor policy for me to knuckle too much to him, although in those days a locomotive engineer was a much more important functionary than he is now, when the woods are full of them.

Well, at last we got our train and got out on the road. We didn't have a very heavy train, and I was satisfied that I could keep her hot without any trouble, and so I could, if he hadn't worked against me in every way. He would let her blow all her steam and water away, until he struck a heavy grade, and then put on his pump full head, and drown her, running the steam down so that we "stalled" and had to "double" up every little hill, and thereby "laid out" the "fast mail" fifteen minutes — an unpardonable sin.

He also "dropped her down a notch" for me, so that she threw a constant stream of sky-rockets out of her stack, and, as I told the master mechanic when he had me on the carpet the next day, a steam shovel couldn't have kept coal in her that night.

Consequently we ran out of fuel before reaching the end of the division, and had to stop at the freight coaling-station and coal up — a thing that had never happened to that train before.

That was a tough run for me, and I found out the reason for it afterwards. Old Joe had powerful influence in high quarters, which made him, to a certain extent, independent of the master mechanic, so that he did pretty much as he pleased, and, being of a low, mean disposition, he pleased to abuse everybody who came in his way; and as nobody came so much in his way as his fireman, he made it so disagreeable for that unfortunate, that several of them had left the road to get away from him, and he had got several others discharged.

When I, a perfect stranger, gave him "sass," he knew that he could lay out the whole road safely by blaming it on me, as it would hardly pay the master mechanic to say anything to him.

All the firemen feared him, and he knew it; so, on this particular occasion, when it became known that Joe's fireman was sick, all the others made it a point to be away from home when the caller made his rounds with orders to call the first man he found off duty.

It was to this combination of circumstances that I owed my job — such as it was. For the first time in his life, I suppose, he got a fireman who had the audacity to talk back to him — to him, Joseph H. Grinnell. Who ever heard of such a thing? Is it any wonder that he determined to cut short my career on that road?

The first time she "dropped her bundle," — which occurred less than half way up the first hill, and before we had gone five miles on our way, — he shut her off, slammed the reverse lever down in the corner with a bang, and, folding his arms, leaned back in his seat, and ripped out the most horrible string of profanity I ever heard, every word of which was a curse at me personally.

I, being a stranger on the road, and not having the fear of old Joe's displeasure properly engrafted on my mind, waited until he got through; then, stepping over to his side, I grabbed him roughly by the shoulder, and twisting him half round on his seat, I said: —

"See here, you foul-mouthed old beast, I've got something to say to *you* now. In the first place, it's your fault and not mine that we're stalled here, because you don't know your business a little bit; where I came from they wouldn't give you a job wheeling ashes out to the dump; and now one thing more, if you open your head to me again while I am on this engine, to say one word, good, bad, or indifferent, I'll split you wide open with this shovel, and if you have any doubt about it, you can satisfy yourself right away."

He didn't say another word to me; but as I said before, the trip was a record-breaker. We got to the end of the division nine hours late, had four hours lay over, and returned, repeating the performance even worse than on the up trip; for, as part of this run occurred during the forenoon, when the inward-bound passenger trains were thick on the road, he managed to lay out three of them.

Before we started on the return trip, the conductor came up to the engine while I was taking water, and said, —

"Say, young feller, the head braky tells me that you set old Joe's packin' out for him in mighty good shape last night. Is that so?"

"Oh, I don't know," said I. "Why?"

"Why? Well, I'll tell you why: because if you did, you've made a friend of every man on the division except Joe himself; and as you couldn't make a friend of him anyway, that's no loss. But, of course, I s'pose you know you're discharged; no man could lay the whole road out the way you did and go out again. But don't you be in any hurry to leave town; for maybe some of us can do something for you, and, at any rate, if you ever want any assistance from anybody on this road, all you've got to do is to say that you are the man that made old Joe Grinnell take water, and the boys won't be able to do enough for you."

When we got back, we both got off the engine, and found the round-house foreman waiting for us. He said the master mechanic wanted to see us both in the office at once, so in we went and reported ourselves.

"Well, Mr. Grinnell," said the master mechanic,

"I have a report here from the division superintendent, in which he informs me that the road wasn't big enough for the 227 last trip. What was the matter with her?"

"Nawthin'," said Grinnell.

"Nothing? What do you mean by that? Something must have been the matter."

"Yes, somethin' was the matter, an' a d—d sight the matter too. Look here, Mr. Seely, I want you to understand that the 227 is a first-class engine in every respect, an' that I'm a first-class engineer; but Phelps has got a notion of fishin' up all sorts of canallers, an' truck-drivers, an' sendin' 'em out to fire for me, an' I'm jist about sick of it, 'n' don't want no more."

"Do you mean to tell me, then, that you laid out the whole road just because the fireman didn't suit you?"

"No, I don't. What I mean to say is, that I didn't hev no fireman; only a cowboy that never fired an engine before, an' threatened to split me wide open with the scoop jest because I told him he'd hev to keep her hot, or we'd never git there."

"Did you threaten Mr. Grinnell?" said Mr. Seely to me.

"Yes, sir," said I.

"Oho! you did, hey? Is that the way firemen talk to their engineers where you came from?"

"No, sir," said I. "But our engineers were men, while this old brute is a —"

"There! there! that will do. I don't want any

quarrelling in my office; you can call in to-morrow and get your time."

So here I was discharged again. It was very discouraging, but then I could expect nothing else, for Joe was an old engineer on the road, and I was what? Merely a straggler that had been picked up in an emergency.

Right here is as good a place as any to make a few remarks concerning the relations existing between engineers and firemen, also in regard to the status of the fireman himself.

No fireman can keep an engine "hot," except with the strictest coöperation on the part of the engineer. In order that the engine shall steam, it is imperative that the engineer shall cut his steam off as short as possible, and run his pump according to certain rules well known to the fraternity. In other words, it is no trouble at all to the engineer to "knock out" the best fireman that ever handled a shovel.

Did you ever see the fireman of any train that you ever rode on? Probably not. You frequently see the engineer, and always the conductor and brakemen; but the fireman is seldom seen, and never heard of, except when he gets killed or hurt in a wreck; and yet in some respects he is the most important man on the train.

Not only do all engineers invariably depend on him to perform many of the duties properly belonging to themselves, but he it is who bends his back, and hustles to make steam to get the train in on time, frequently with miserable fuel and an engine that ought to be in the scrap-heap. When time is lost for the want of steam, it is on the fireman's devoted head that the wrath of the engineer, master mechanic, and superintendent falls; no excuse being accepted, even though it be evident to anybody that the coal is 70 per cent slate, and the valves and pistons blow like sieves.

Though all the train-despatchers, brass-bound conductors, and engineers do their level best, no train can make time or break a record unless the grimy, unheard of, and unthought-about fireman, down there in his black hole, knows his business, and *does* it.

Yet no praise comes to him for the good run, though he is the one man on the train who has labored and sweated to make it, and to whose skill and knowledge it is largely due.

Well, there was no use crying over spilt milk, so I went to the round-house, washed up, and then went to get something to eat. I ran across the conductor, who was bound on the same errand, and told him what had occurred in the master mechanic's office, and also gave him a short account of myself. I found that he knew my former conductor, and had heard of the wreck which was the cause of all of us getting discharged. He was quite friendly and invited me to sleep in his caboose during its stay at that end of the division, and get acquainted with the boys. "For," said he, "railroad men when looking for a job are not apt to be very rich, and there's no use of paying for lodgings while the yard is half full of cabooses."

I accepted his invitation thankfully and found that I was quite a hero. The men took delight in introducing me as the fellow who had bearded old Joe in his cab, and yet survived to tell the tale.

They also liked to hear me tell of my experience in what is still remembered by old railroaders as the Brookdale disaster.

The result of their hospitality was, that three days passed before I returned to the master mechanic's office for the bill of my time. On leaving the office I ran across Mr. Phelps, who asked me to accompany him to the round-house. He took me away round out of sight and hearing, behind a big freight engine, and asked what was the trouble between Grinnell and me.

I told him all that happened on the trip, but before I got through he said, "Never mind all that; I want to know what it was that you said to him."

When I told him, a broad smile spread over his face, as he asked,—

"Did you tell him that?"

"Yes, sir," said I.

"What did he say?"

"Not a word to me from that time to this."

"Haw! haw! haw! by George, that's good!" And he leaned up against the tender and laughed, and slapped himself till the dust flew out of his overalls in clouds.

"I'd have been willin' to lose a month's pay to have seen ole Joe then," said he. "Say, young feller, I can't give you a job firin' just yet; Joe's queered you for a bit, but I'll tell you what I'll do. I'll set you to wipin', an' give you the first chance. What do you say?"

"How long will it be before you can give me a job firing?" said I.

"Oh! I can't tell that; nobody can. Maybe in thirty days, maybe in six months; but you're sure of a job sooner or later, an' in the meantime you can git acquainted with the men an' engines, an' that's better than to start in somewhere bran new and git dumped again, ain't it?"

I told him I thought it might be in some respects; still I didn't care to wipe engines, as that is the very lowest rung in the ladder, besides being extremely dirty and disagreeable work.

He assured me, however, that both the master mechanic and himself, as well as nearly all the engineers on the road, had begun as wipers. He said that was the proper way for a man to learn any trade, to begin at the bottom; and in fine, he said so much, and seemed so anxious to have me take the job, that I accepted, and have never regretted it to this day.

For fifteen months I wiped engines, turned the table, shoveled ashes, washed out boilers and tanks, helped the machinists to lug and lift, and in fact did all manner of the dirtiest and hardest work that has to be done about a railroad round-house. For the wipers are everybody's helpers. Is a particularly hard job to be done, get one of the wipers to do it; if a sewer gets clogged, send a wiper in to clear it; and who ever heard of a wiper complaining? They seem to glory in and thrive on dirt.

During those fifteen months I became, from constant association, perfectly familiar with all the outward and visible parts of the locomotive, and I saw them taken to pieces by the mechanics, and as I was blessed with a good-sized bump of inquisitiveness, I also learned enough of the mysterious properties of the slide valve to enable me to take part in the deeply erudite discussions which frequently took place among the firemen. I became — in my own opinion, at any rate — an authority on "lap" and "lead," "compression," "expansion," and "cut off."

There is no other way in which a green man can learn so well and so thoroughly every detail of the machine, as he can by going over it daily, wiping all its parts carefully, and observing what each one is for.

The wipers are severe critics of the engineers; they know whose engine is always in first-class order, nuts and bolts all in place and tight, wedges never down, and everything where it ought to be.

It seemed as if some engineers depended on the wipers to look out for broken spring leaves and hangers, cracked equalizers and eccentric straps, and nearly everything else; but there were some who looked their engines over with the greatest care, and one of these was old Joe Grinnell. He didn't want any help from anybody, and was quite free in saying so, too; but I was lucky enough to discover something that he had missed one day, and it did me a world of good.

He couldn't help seeing me about the round-house, as I was nearly always at work on his engine when he came to get her ready, and see that the repairs he had reported were done properly before going out, but he never took the slightest notice of me. I was too far beneath him to be even worth d—ing.

The engine truck was a part that was assigned to me to wipe, and one day I noticed that the male centre casting was broken in such a way that but one bolt held it at all, and that very slightly. I supposed, of course, that he had reported it, and expected every minute to see the men come along with the jacks and jack her up to put in a new one; for though there is a king-pin down through both castings, still no man would ever trust to that alone, for she would be apt, in rounding some curve, to shear it off, and, shooting off at a tangent, leave the track.

What was my surprise, then, as the time drew near for her to leave the house, to see that no attempt was made to repair the damage, until at last the hostler took her out across the table. I had been long enough in the round-house now to get the hang of things pretty well, so I hunted up Mr. Phelps and told him what I had discovered on the 227.

"Is that so?" said he; "are you sure?"

"Yes, sir," said I; "there's no doubt about it."

We walked rapidly round the house and came to the hook on which the machinists hang the engineers' work reports after finishing the job and marking them O. K.

He hunted the hook over until he found the 227's report signed, Grinnell, O. K'd., and signed by the man who had done the work. There were several little petty jobs reported, but not a word about the centre casting.

Mr. Phelps' eyes sparkled with pleasure, as he saw that old Joe had tripped at last.

"D—n him," said he; "if there was only him to think of, I'd let him go, — 'twould be an almighty good way to git rid of him; but there are good men who would have to suffer too."

From where we stood we could see Joe oiling around; no time was to be lost, for we didn't want him to discover it, though, even if he did, it would be too late now to save himself from censure — still we desired to catch him as foul as possible.

Turning to me, Mr. Phelps said, "I'll get the old man out, an' walk him past the engine, an' you be close by, an' just as we get to Joe, you tell him his centre castin's broke."

"All right, sir," said I, and away he went post haste after the master mechanic, while I sauntered out in the direction of the 227.

Joe was oiling his engine truck boxes, and I was in a flutter, for fear he might look underneath and

"'Mr. Grinnell, your engine truck centre casting is broken all to pieces.'" — p. 83.

discover it for himself; but fortunately another engineer came along just then and engaged him in conversation, thereby distracting his attention.

Directly I saw Mr. Seely and Mr. Phelps coming rapidly in our direction from the office, I got within about ten feet of old Joe, and just as they were passing, called out loud enough for everybody to hear:

"Mr. Grinnell, your engine truck centre casting is broken all to pieces, and just about ready to fall off."

Joe's face was like a thunder-cloud as he told me to mind my own d—d business, if I had any.

The officials had heard my report, and stopping short, Mr. Seely asked Joe what was the matter with his centre casting.

"Nawthin'," said Joe; "only this wiper's found a mare's nest. I guess I'm competent to look after my own engine without any help from the wipers."

Mr. Seely, however, looked under the engine himself, and seeing that I was right, ordered her back into the house, and a spare engine got ready in a hurry, and then he read the riot act to Mr. Joseph H. Grinnell in a manner that the oldest "plug-puller" on the road had never heard equalled.

He told him that he was the most ignorant, useless, and conceited fool he had ever seen; he told him he was neither an engineer, a man, mouse, monkey, nor anything else. He said it was only his influence at headquarters, and not his ability, that had caused the road to be cumbered with his useless carcass so long as it had.

At first Joe answered back pretty stiffly, but as he knew he was dead wrong, he couldn't say much.

The old man had him just where he had wanted to get him for years, and he did him up brown.

The engineers, firemen, wipers, and in fact everybody about the place, came running from all directions to help hear old Joe get his tongue-lashing. The downfall of that old brute was most gorgeous, and satisfactory to everybody — except Joe.

As a grand finale, the old man, after calling him everything but a "first-class engineer," sent him home for ten days, charged with *incompetency*.

After that Mr. Joseph could seldom go near the round-house without hearing from behind some far-off engine the derisive cry of "centre casting," "mare's nest," "wipers' reports," or something equally suggestive of the day when he got what he had been so long aching for.

CHAPTER VIII

CUTTING A CONDUCTOR IN TWO — FIRING FOR "POUNDERS" — OLD POP FICKETT — A LEAP FOR LIFE — PHEW! — PROMOTED TO THE LEFT SIDE — DISCHARGED — APPEAL TO HEADQUARTERS

THE next morning when I came to work, Mr. Phelps told me to go home again, and return at 6 P.M. to relieve a fireman on one of the switch engines. My wiping days were now over, and once more I found myself on the left side of a locomotive. During those fifteen months of wiping I had come to regard the fireman's position as being little less unattainable than the president's; so having earned my job, I appreciated it, and felt all the pride of ownership as I stepped on to the foot-board of that old switch engine.

I took an immediate and fierce hold of the brass work, for I was determined to have the cleanest engine in the yard; but when the engineer saw what I was about, he said: "Say! ye d—d fool, what ye tryin' ter do? this ain't no cannon-ball engine. Set down there 'n' watch out fer signals!" Being extremely sensitive to ridicule, the jeering tone in which he spoke was like a cold douche to my ardent ambition, and I very soon learned to content myself with the regular routine work, without attempting to introduce radical reforms into the yard engine service. On the second day, the engineer asked me if I thought I could handle her. I said, I guessed so, and stepping out from alongside the boiler, he said, "All right, then; get hold o' this bat, an' let's see ye shape yerself."

I was somewhat nervous at first. It startled me to feel her go the instant that I touched the throttle, and though I knew perfectly *how* she ought to be handled, yet I found it confusing when I came to do it myself. The throttle, reverse lever, and brake seemed to be in each other's way, and I couldn't find them with my hands without looking for them — an act that is rankly unprofessional. Then again, I would catch myself just in the act of giving her steam, when I should have reversed her first, calling forth profane and jeering remarks from the engineer, which were extremely mortifying. The engineer stayed with me about an hour, watching me sharply, and giving me lots of advice. I took it as I was in duty bound; but as it was none of it news to me, I paid but little attention, resolving that if I ever had the chance I would do these things to suit myself; but, of course, I didn't dare let him know that. I soon gained confidence, and as I kept a sharp lookout for signals, and obeyed them promptly, the engineer — satisfied that I could do the work — stepped off and went into the yard-master's office to "chin." He had not been off the engine ten minutes when I cut the conductor in two; or, rather, he was accidentally cut in two, partly owing to his own fault.

He undertook to make a "double cut," that is, to cut off two sections of the moving train, and send each into its own proper switch without stopping. When properly done, it is a neat manœuvre, and a great time-saver. There should be a man at each switch — one to pull the pin, and one to watch the performance and give signals to the engineer. The pin may be pulled on the first section before commencing to back, then the pin-puller stands by to make the second cut. The engine starts back until there is way enough on the first cut to carry it into its switch; then at a signal the engineer shuts off, and the dead engine acting as a drag holds back the main part of the train, while the cut-off cars roll on ahead to their switch, which the man who is stationed there opens, allowing them to run in, and closes it after them. The engineer, on signal, now gives her another jerk back, the pin-puller pulls the pin, and when there is way enough on the second cut to carry it to its destination, the same performance is gone through with again, this time the whole of the remaining train and engine passing over the closed switch to its destination further up the yard.

With men enough — provided there is no grade to stop the cars from rolling — cars could be sent into all the switches along the line, without the engine stopping at all; but in this case the conductor only had one man, and when he told him what he intended to do, the brakey remonstrated, saying: "Ye'll have them all over the d—d carpet." The conductor, however, told him to mind his own business, and do as he was ordered. As it turned out, the brakey was right; for he did spread them all over the carpet, and lost his life besides. He told the brakeman to open the first switch, and then run to the next, saying that he would close it himself after pulling the pin. But when he ran in a hurry to close it, he stumbled over the end of a tie, so that before he got it closed, the forward truck of the leading car had entered the siding, and the switch being closed the cars went off the track. Seeing them going in all directions, he desired to set a brake to hold them when, in jumping up between two flat cars, one corner rose above the other, and shearing across it clipped him in two, as a lady snips a thread with her scissors.

The engineer was discharged for allowing me to handle the engine, and for many a night after that I saw the poor man in my dreams. He had been looking straight in my eyes, when his light went out.

I fired nearly four years; and though firing is the hardest kind of work, I look back to those four years as the happiest of my life.

I never came across quite such another crank as old Joe Grinnell, for as a rule the engineers were fine fellows. Every man jack of them, having served his apprenticeship at the scoopshovel, realized the drawbacks and discomforts of the fireman's position, and tried to make it as endurable as possible.

Some, while meaning well, had failed during their apprenticeship to learn from their engineers how to run and feed (pump) the machine to the best advantage, so they made hard work for the fireman to keep steam. Those we called "pounders," and as a rule they were the very ones who would take no hints from their firemen, but instantly became dignified and talked loftily about how *I* pump and run *my* engine.

Shortly after I was appointed, I was sent to fire for old Pop Fickett. He was a jolly old soul, easy-going as an old shoe, and would often on a cold night get down and fire himself for a dozen or twenty miles to get warm, while I sat on his seat and played engineer, blowing for crossings, and watching the water.

Old Pop was a hard man to fire for, because he was a pounder; but I hadn't been long enough at the business to know that, so I shovelled away for dear life and was ignorant and happy.

One trip Pop reported sick, and an extra engineer took her out. As a rule, firemen hate to see an extra man get on the engine, as he has different ways from the man you are used to, and railroad men of all degrees get set in their ways and don't like to have them disturbed.

This extra man, however, was a genuine and pleasant surprise to me. With old Pop at the throttle I always had to bend my back as soon as he pulled her out and keep the shovel and the firebox door on the swing as regular as the pendulum of a clock.

No need to hook the fire; for as Pop said, he'd keep it from freezing up on me, and so he did too; for I wouldn't have a chance to stop shovelling until he shut her off. No need to worry myself by looking at the steam-gauge; for as Pop said again, he could take care of all the steam I could make.

There were two coaling stations on the division, each about twenty miles from either terminus, for the convenience of engines that needed more coal to take them in. We never passed them,—indeed, we sometimes had trouble to reach them,—although Pop had sideboards put on the tender, saying he liked to have plenty of coal; and when other engineers bragged about how many water-plugs they passed, and how many cars they hauled without taking coal, Pop would remark sagely that "he allus liked to have coal an' water enough,"—and he did too.

Well, when the extra man started I began as usual to "ladle in the lampblack" until we were about five miles out, when he called me up to him and asked me if there was a hole through the front end of the firebox.

"No," said I. "Why?"

"What is the trouble, then? Is there somebody buried back there, an' you're trying to dig him out?"

I stared at him, wondering what he was talking about. Seeing that I didn't understand, he said, "For Heaven's sake, man, get up there on your seat an' sit down! I never saw anybody shovel coal like you do; you've got enough in there to run to the next water-plug now. I can't put any more water into her till we get there; so crack your door an' let's have a smoke."

I did as he told me to; and yet, though I saw by the gauge that we had, as the boys say, "a hundred an' enough," I was worried; and at last, when I could stand it no longer, fearing that my fire would go entirely out, I stepped down and picked up my scoop again.

"Say," said he, "hand me that scoop a minute."

I did so, wondering what he wanted of it.

He threw it on the foot-board in front of him, and told me if I didn't sit down and rest myself until we got to the water-plug he would report me for wasting the company's fuel.

That trip was a revelation to me. We not only ran by half the water-plugs and the coal station, but made the run in two hours' less time than usual, arriving with nearly half a tank of coal left, although we had our regular train of forty-five loads.

The next day I asked him how it was done. He took me to his side of the cab and showed me a notch in the quadrant that was worn smooth and bright.

"That," said he, "is the notch Pop runs her in." Then he showed me where he ran her, and gave me the most lucid explanation of early cutting off and running expansively, and of its effect on the coal-pile and water-tank, that I had ever heard.

Pop was laid up a week with rheumatism, and during that week I gained several pounds in weight. I had such an easy time of it that, although I was very fond of the old man, I dreaded to see him come back, and said as much to the engineer.

"Why don't you tell him how to run her," said he. "Pop's a good old feller. He won't get mad; and even if he does, you'd be a blamed fool to keep heaving coal in there for him to throw out the stack. I wouldn't do it, an' don't you."

Well, at last the day came when the old man returned to work. He looked poorly, and I could hardly find it in my heart to speak to him on a subject which I knew to be a delicate one, for he was a very old engineer, and had been running just that way probably long before I ever thought of railroading.

Still, I had lots of sympathy for my own back. So at last I broached the subject, before we started — I would have no chance afterward — and made up my mind to fight it out with him if necessary.

I spoke rather diffidently, but told him the whole story, to which he listened very patiently, and when I got through, he said, —

"My boy, I don't want to break your back. I know there's something in what you say, for I've had firemen kick before, but none of them in such a decent way as you have; now I'll tell you something that no man on this road knows but me. I am a machinist by trade, and never fired but six months in my life. When this road opened, I had a little influence and got a job; all I asked for was a job, but as I had a letter from a big man, and applied to the mechanical department, I was presumed to be an engineer, and given an engine at once. Of course, I wasn't fool enough to decline, and I've been running here ever since. That's twenty years ago, and you're the first fireman I ever had that I would trust enough to tell that to. Now, show me how Laws ran her, and by gum, I'll do the same; then we'll see if we can't run by water-plugs and coal stations as well as some others."

I showed him, and away we went. At first he was afraid she wouldn't make time, cut back so fine, but when he saw how she was going past the stations, he was as pleased as a child with a new toy. When we neared the first water-plug, he sent me back to measure the water. We had nearly half a tank, and he wanted to stop; but I assured him that it was perfectly safe to go on, and so it proved.

He was as pleased as Punch when we wheeled into the end of the division after the fastest trip he had ever made in all those twenty years, and never relapsed into his old style of running, and for the remainder of my time with him no fireman on the road had an easier time of it than I.

We met with the usual mishaps that occur to freight trains everywhere. But as I shall have enough to tell about those that happened to me after I get to running, I will only relate one here.

We had on the fast freight, a light time table train of perishable goods; for Pop had made such a record for speed lately, that being an old and in all respects a first-class man, they had given him this train. We had (or supposed we had) a clear track before us, and he was wheeling them for dear life.

I was hooking up my fire (I had to do that now occasionally since the new style of running had come into vogue), when suddenly he shut her off and blew brakes. I couldn't see a thing after looking into the bright fire, but I heard him yell, "Git out of here!"

You may be sure that I had learned to jump long before this; so without waiting for a written invitation, and not wishing to get off on my side and be rolled over and torn by the ties and rails of the opposite track, I shut my teeth hard and made a flying leap, out into the darkness on the right side as far as I could go, thinking to myself as I went that I hoped I wouldn't strike a telegraph pole — and I didn't.

We were just entering a small country town; an opposing freight train had occasion to cross over to our track, so the engineer sent the head man out with orders to let us pass (as we were nearly due) and hold all second-class trains after that until he called him in. In a case of this kind, it is understood that the engineer and conductor will clear the track in time to allow first-class trains to pass; that is, the flagman has orders to hold only *second-class* trains, *i.e. freight*. The flagman was lighting his pipe and listening to some story of the fireman's, so that he didn't notice what the engineer said about our train; so when he saw a second-class train coming, he flagged, and as we were coming at a good gait, he flagged furiously.

Pop, seeing the headlight, supposed of course they were crossed over (as they had a perfect right to be), and fearing he couldn't stop in the distance he had, horsed her over, and we jumped.

The station agent had been buying manure from the farmers all winter and stacking it in a huge pile alongside the track.

As it was offensive to the public, he had orders from the superintendent to get rid of it as fast as possible. So as it was late in the spring when we made our eventful jump, the pile was about half gone, and as there had been a good deal of rain for a week past, the immediate vicinity of it was a wet, soggy, malodorous locality, thoroughly fermented with the distillation from the heap, covered with its leavings and numerous dark brown puddles. Into this I went, and Pop after me. I landed on my feet, but immediately pitched over and ploughed into it. I don't know how Pop landed, but when the conductor asked him afterwards if he fell, he said he fell seven times.

At any rate, we ploughed and rolled, wallowed and spluttered, in our fragrant bath to more than our hearts' content, — much more, — until our momentum having expended itself, we crawled dripping, half blinded and strangled, up the bank, to find our train stopped and no harm done except to ourselves and our feelings.

Perhaps that flagman didn't get a blessing! Pop wanted to go back and kill him after he heard the engineer's explanation.

Fortunately it was a water station, so we took turns letting the water run on each other (nobody else would come near us) until we had cleansed ourselves as well as we could, and then got on the engine and went on. But for a long time it was a standing joke of Pop's to ask me not to come any nearer than was necessary please, and I would reply, "For the Lord's sake, do you expect *anybody* to get any nearer to you than they are obliged to? Phew! why don't you mortgage your farm and buy a carload of 'Florida water'?"

Having served a good spell on freight, I was beginning to hanker for promotion to the left side of a passenger train. Then indeed I could feel that I had a good job. Every day I should know just what my duties were, and though the engineer might not be as genial and companionable as Pop, I was willing to risk the change. They were paid by the mile, and they could see us fellows lying in the side track with our old freight trains, losing time, while they went wheeling by us, forty and fifty miles an hour. They could go over the division and pass us again sometimes on the same trip. They of course earned much more money, and did it much more easily. I should then come into immediate contact with the oldest and most experienced firemen on the road, and should begin to move in circles where promotion was discussed as a matter of immediate personal interest.

About this time, an engineer who had left the road a couple of years before returned, and was appointed travelling engineer by the master mechanic. We soon found that he had full authority to hire engineers to fill vacancies, and that he improved his opportunities. A new branch connecting with an important mining and manufacturing locality was opened, calling for half a dozen more engineers. The firemen had been longing for the opening, and figuring for the past three years, on who would be promoted; but when the time drew near, it was observed that several new engineers were riding on the engines, learning the road. The firemen became alarmed at once, and discussed the matter quite freely. The engineers took a hand in, and notified us that if we cared to keep our jobs, we had better attend to our own business and let the officers run the road to suit themselves. As they had the ear of their former comrade, the travelling engineer, this may have accounted for their enthusiasm in upholding the management.

I became intensely interested in the controversy; and though I could not expect to be promoted at this time, yet I saw that if the engineers were all to be hired, our chances of ever running on that road were slim indeed. As no one seemed to have any idea of demanding better treatment from the company, or to consider that we had anything that could be termed *rights* in the matter, I made it my business to preach a new doctrine to my companions, and after much patient argument, succeeded in convincing many of them that we were not by any means subsisting on the company's charity. I said that we were as necessary to the operation of the road as the locomotives themselves, and when some one would jeeringly ask if I thought the road would stop in case I quit, I told him it was not the individual who was necessary, that I realized any one's services could be dispensed with from the president down, but the vacancies must be filled by some one, hence I claimed that what was essential to the operation of the road in the instance under discussion was *firemen, some* firemen — if not us, then others; therefore, being necessary to the operation of the road, it was not unreasonable in us to claim some consideration at the hands of the management, and to endeavor to establish certain rights for ourselves. Here, again, the engineers laughed at us. They said they could run the engines with shoeblacks, or farmers, as firemen; but I told them that didn't invalidate my argument, as all I contended was, that they must have *firemen*.

I succeeded in making myself very unpopular with the engineers; but as I had infused new life and hope into the firemen, I didn't care much about that. I finally got three of the oldest men, three who had felt sure of promotion, to go with me as a committee to the travelling engineer and ask that the firemen's

"We found the gentleman sitting with his feet cocked up on his desk, smoking." — p. 99.

rights to promotion be recognized, provided I would agree to do all the talking, which I was perfectly willing to do, as I thought I could advance such a convincing argument that he would be obliged to fall into our view of the matter.

So one fine day I marshalled my committee in the anteroom of the master mechanic's office, resolved to beard the lion in his den. We were all trembling in our shoes, at the audacity of our action, and wished that we hadn't been so valiant; however, it was too late now to turn back, as all the firemen knew what we were about, and a number were waiting in the round-house to receive our report. So in we went, our caps in our hands, and asked to see Mr. Hussey. A clerk stepped into his office, and returning directly, bade us enter.

We found the gentleman sitting with his feet cocked up on his desk, smoking; we walked round so as to face him, and I asked, in a voice which I fear was slightly tremulous, if we could speak to him. He gave me a quick, disagreeable glance from his cold, gray eye, and answered in a most discouraging manner, "Ya—as, go on."

After once having broken the ice, I found but little difficulty in talking. I stated the case to him, as I had done to the boys dozens of times already. I told him that we based our claim to recognition, on the ground that firemen were a necessary adjunct to a railroad; therefore we felt that as we had performed our duties satisfactorily, which I claimed was proven by our retention in the service, we believed we were entitled to some slight consideration, that we didn't wish to fire all our lives, and believed we were just as capable of becoming engineers as any one else had ever been, and, in short, I asked him bluntly to fill the vacancies which would soon occur, by promoting firemen instead of hiring engineers.

When I got through he gave me another one of those wicked leers, and said, "Are you done?"

"Yes, sir," said I.

"Got no instructions for the master mechanic or superintendent?"

"No, sir; we've got no instructions for anybody; we are simply asking for what we think we are entitled to."

"Oho! you're mighty mild all of a sudden! Well, now look here, my young agitator, I've had my eye on you for some time, and I've heard a good deal about you, too; going round among the firemen, talking and criticising my business. You want what you're entitled to, hey? Well, you shall have it, and that's a bill of your time. Does any of the rest of you want what he's entitled to?"

Glancing hastily at the boys, I saw they were badly rattled; so, thinking it useless to sacrifice any more of them, I told him that I was the only one to blame for the action we had taken, and got them out of the office as quickly as I could.

We were no sooner outside than two of my gallant supporters sneaked off to the round-house, thankful to have escaped with their lives; but one, Frank

Manly, a smart, bright young fellow of about twenty-one, slightly red-headed, tall, and straight as an arrow, Manly by name, and manly by nature, brought his right fist down in his left palm with a bang, and swore that it was an infernal shame. "I'll tell you what I'll do, Joe," said he; "I'll go back in that office, and yank that d—d hound out from behind his desk, and mop up the floor with him; d—n him! I always hated him, and would like no better fun than to give him an almighty good licking, an' I can do it, too."

He turned to go in again, but I caught him by the arm, and told him not to be a fool; for while I had no doubt that he could lick Hussey, he would not only lose his job, but probably get himself locked up besides.

"Ah! who cares for their old job? D'ye think I want to stay down in that black hole, an' ladle lamp-black into these ole man-eaters all my life, so's he can hire all his drunken friends, that can't run anywhere else? No, sir, I wouldn't fire another scoopful of coal on this road, if I had to go hod-carrying for a living!"

While he was ranting in this manner, I had gradually drawn him away from the office door, and we strolled up the street, discussing the matter loudly and angrily; for we were both well riled. Finally Frank asked me what I intended to do.

"What can I do, but hunt another job? I'm discharged here."

He walked along in silence for several minutes, thinking deeply, then, looking up, he said, —

"Don't you do it; he had no right to discharge you for that. I'll tell you what we'll do; it wouldn't do any good to go to the master mechanic, because he'd uphold Hussey; and the super's no better. I won't fire on the blame road any more, as long as that's to be the rule; so let's you and me go straight to the general manager. They say he's a mighty fine old fellow; been all through the mill himself, an' believes in giving the boys a fair show. We've got nothing to lose, anyway, so he can't hurt us. What do you say?"

I told him I was willing; so the next day we marched into the general manager's office, as large as life, and at once ran foul of his very inquisitive private secretary, who wouldn't admit us until he found out just what our business was. I didn't think it advisable to tell him, but Frank said it was no secret, and blurted it all out. Then he wanted to know why we bothered the general manager with such matters, why didn't we go to the master mechanic or the superintendent, and so on, until Frank, losing his temper, told him we didn't want to see anybody, but would settle the matter elsewhere, and off we started. At this the fussy little old fellow changed his tactics, called us back, advised us not to get excited, and said he would find out if the gentleman would see us.

He presently returned from the inner sanctum

and told us to be seated, that the general manager was very busy, but would see us directly.

In about half an hour a man came out, and we were told to step inside. Neither of us had ever seen the general manager before, so we were pleasantly surprised to find that august person a very mild-mannered and affable gentleman. He welcomed us cordially, asked us to be seated, and read from a slip of paper, "Two of the firemen."

"It should be ex-firemen, sir," said I, "we are no longer employed on your road."

He raised his eyebrows slightly and said, "In that case I hardly see how you can have any business with me. It was on the supposition that you were employees that I granted you this audience."

I asked if he would allow us to state our case.

"Certainly," said he. "Proceed; but be as brief as you can, for my time is valuable."

I told him the whole story: how we had been disappointed in our promotion, how we had respectfully protested to Mr. Hussey, and I, as spokesman, had been peremptorily discharged. He seemed interested, and heard me through without interruption, and when I had finished, he asked: "Who is Mr. Hussey?" I told him.

"And he discharged you both?"

"No, sir," said Frank. "I wasn't discharged; but as I don't intend to fire all my life, I have quit."

"And quite right too. If I knew that I had a man on my road that hadn't ambition enough to aspire to the highest position on it, I'd discharge him myself. Now you boys understand that you have made a grave charge to me against your superior officer. If I bring him here, will you repeat the charges in his presence?"

"Yes, sir, we will."

"Have you any witnesses?"

"We have the other two firemen who were on the committee; but perhaps they wouldn't care to testify."

"What are their names?"

We told him their names, and he took them down. He then told us to be in his office again at ten o'clock next morning. Frank asked if we should notify our witnesses to appear. "They will be notified," said he, "and will be here, or I am very much mistaken." I remarked that one of them was to go out at 4 P.M. "Ah!" said he, "that's well thought of." He then told his clerk to tell the master mechanic's office to relieve fireman Voorhees until further orders: and dismissed us, with a warning to talk to no one about the matter.

When we got outside, Frank almost danced for joy. "I tell you, Joe," said he, "we've got that pug-nosed Hussey just where we want him. I'll bet you that if it ever comes his turn to entertain a firemen's committee again, he'll know how to receive 'em a blame sight better than he did last time. Bully for the old man! he's a brick! I hope he'll discharge Mr. Great-I-am Hussey. It would serve him glad; he'd know how it feels himself, then."

Back we went to the boarding-house, and kept out of sight as much as possible; but we were unable to escape some questioning, though when asked what we were going to do now, we answered that we had not yet made up our minds.

The next day we arrived at the office on time, where we found Mr. Hussey, who paid not the slightest attention to us and our two committeemen, who were in what Frank called a "blue funk," wondering what was to be done to them. The general manager arrived shortly after us, bowed comprehensively to the crowd, said, "Good-morning, gentlemen; step inside, please," and when we were all in, asked us to be seated.

"Now," said he, "which is Mr. Hussey?"

"I am Mr. Hussey," said that gentleman, disguising as much as possible his naturally surly manner, out of deference to his superior officer.

"I have received a very grave charge, Mr. Hussey, from one, or perhaps I should say two, of our firemen, one of whom you have discharged, as I understand, for having preferred a request on behalf of himself and others. Is that correct?"

"I discharged that feller," said Hussey, indicating me by a jerk of his head, "because he's an agitator: he's been organizin' the firemen, an' tryin' ter make trouble on the road. I should have discharged him at the first chance, anyway; so, when he came into my office an' tried to dictate to me who I should hire an' who I should promote, I let 'im go. I don't want no firemen, nor engineers neither, dictatin' to me, an' I won't have it!"

"Be seated a moment, please," said the general manager.

He then called the members of the committee up, one after another, and, after warning them to be careful to state the exact facts, drew from them the conversation that had passed between Hussey and me in the office. He asked Hussey if it was correct, and he admitted that it was. He then said that it was his wish that all employees on the road should be considered as standing in the line of promotion in their several departments; that he had always supposed such to be the case, and was surprised to find it otherwise, as he had certainly made his views known on that subject. He said that promotions should be governed by seniority of service, unless the senior employee could be shown to be unfit for the position; favoritism he would not tolerate under any disguise whatsoever. He gave Mr. Hussey a very plain lecture on the autocratic position which he had assumed toward us, saying that he desired all employees to discuss among themselves matters pertaining to their own interests, and to suggest such changes as they thought would be beneficial to themselves, guaranteeing that all such questions should receive his personal attention, and any concessions that could be made without injury to the interests of the road he would gladly make. He told us that any employee could always obtain an audience with him, and said that the right of appeal from the decisions of inferior officers should be the rule while he remained in the company's employ.

He then told Frank and me to return to work, and was about to dismiss us, when Hussey, who had been getting red in the face and showing signs of increasing uneasiness, rose, and said in a somewhat insolent tone, —

"Do you mean to say, Mr. General Manager, that that feller's reinstated over my head?"

"You can call it that, if you choose."

"Well, I'll tell you one thing: I don't care if you're general manager, or what you are, you can't run no railroad that way—"

"There! there!" said the old gentleman, knocking on his desk with a pencil, "that will do. I think I understand you, and let me give you a little piece of advice,—when talking to a gentleman, be as gentlemanly as you can, and when addressing your superior officer, try and remember that a certain modicum of respect is due to his position—"

"Gentleman be d—d!" roared Hussey. "What are ye? Ye're nothin' but an old ex-freight brakeman, an' ye're so d—d old that whatever little sense ye might have had once is all gone now. To blazes with you an' yer ole streak of rust! I wouldn't work on a road that's got such an old woman fool for a general manager, if it was the only road on earth!" And he started for the door just as it was opened by a burly attendant, who quietly, but firmly, and with an air of dexterity which proved familiarity with the method, took Mr. Hussey by the wrist and elbow and escorted him, swearing uproariously, to the outer world.

We bade the general manager good day, thanking him for his kindness, and withdrew. Frank and I kept a little in advance of the others on our return, though they tried to fraternize; but we looked upon them coldly, and so discouraged their advances.

CHAPTER IX

SETTING HUSSEY'S PACKING OUT — THE NEW SUPER — BE CAREFUL BUT MAKE TIME — THE PRICE OF LIBERTY — FIRING FOR SIMPSON — HELL-FIRE JACK AND SECOND FOUR — COLLISION — THE FARMER, THE COW, AND THE FLIP-FLAP — A RUN-AWAY ENGINE

THE results of our interview were very satisfactory. We got rid of Hussey, who spent a month in a drunken celebration of his discharge; pouring out dire threats of vengeance against Frank and me, until Frank ran across him one evening and "set his packing out" so satisfactorily that he left town that same night on a through freight, rather than exhibit his damaged countenance to the intensely unsympathetic gaze of the railroaders; for now that he was shorn of power to either punish or reward, his fine-weather friends fell away, and he found himself decidedly unpopular, so that none sympathized with the fond delusion which he entertained for some time of being sent for and reinstated.

The magnitude of our success dazed and almost frightened us. Our visit to the general manager had been undertaken merely as a forlorn hope, and with hardly any expectation of being granted even an interview. We were lionized by the firemen, and looked upon with sincere dislike by the engineers; as it was for their interest to have all railroads hire engineers. Even old Pop told me, with the utmost gravity, that I might as well quit, and go along with Hussey; for he said the master mechanic would now be down on me for having been instrumental in getting Hussey discharged, and interfering with the management of his department. He predicted that my stay on the road would be very limited, but I remembered what the general manager had said to us about the right of appeal, and made up my mind that if the master mechanic did me an injustice, I would fight it out as I had in the last instance.

I had occasion several times to remember Pop's words; for though I was not discharged, a system of petty annoyances was started against me in the effort to tire me out, so that I would leave of my own accord. It became a frequent occurrence now for me to be called to the office, to receive reprimands and warnings for all sorts of unimportant matters; and as I knew the method pursued on railroads, I understood the meaning of these actions on the master mechanic's part.

A strict record is kept of the service of every employee. A report is filed with the head of the department of all violations of the rules, and the punishments awarded for the same; so that when at any time a serious offence is committed, the superintendent can call for the man's record, and base his decision to a great extent upon it, and as it is a practical impossibility to obey all orders, and at the same time perform one's duty, a prejudiced official can ruin the record of any man. For instance, we got a new superintendent, and like the proverbial new broom, he swept exceedingly clean. He was not a practical railroader, but had been all his life a clerk; however, he succeeded in gaining the good will of the general superintendent who recommended his appointment when a vacancy occurred, and the general manager sanctioned it. The new super lived a dozen miles or so out on the road, where there was a station located down in a hole with sharp curves entering it from both directions. There had been several little wrecks there, caused by trains coming down into the station and hitting others pulling out of the siding, and of course the excuse always was that worm-eaten chestnut "brakes didn't hold," though every one knew that if they came in there under control as they should, they would be able to stop on getting the flag.

The new super published an entirely unnecessary order to the effect that all second-class trains (freight) should come into this place prepared to stop before reaching the switch. One evening while sitting on his piazza he saw a stock train go down there at what *he* thought was a dangerous rate of speed. The next day he had the engineer in his office and *cautioned* him.

The engineer said to him: "I had hauled that train over a hundred miles before you saw it, and knew just what I could do with it. At the rate I was going I would have had no difficulty whatever, in stopping clear of the switch. You want these stock trains to go over the division in six hours, when you know we have got to violate the twenty mile per hour rule to do it, and squeeze out every half minute possible on all such cautionary orders as this; to say nothing of running by slow flags and through yard limits, at a speed that will down us if anything ever goes wrong at any of those places. Yet if we don't make the time you want with these trains, you will take us off, and give them to somebody else. Now what is a man to do?"

He got no direct answer; it isn't policy for a railroad official to answer embarrassing questions of that sort. The superintendent contented himself with warning the engineer to "be careful, very careful; I wouldn't allow you to go out on the head of a train if I didn't know that you are a good careful man, but of course I want you to make time."

The engineer then complained that in five years' running on the road he had never before been called to the office, and had taken great pride in keeping his record clear.

"Yes, I know," said this Daniel come to judgment; "I looked up your record and found that *up to the present* it was clear."

Having got rid of Hussey before he had succeeded in filling all of the vacancies with hired men, a couple of the old firemen were promoted; and their places on passenger trains filled by promoting firemen from the freight department. Although there were three older men than I on freight, one of those promoted was younger, so I went to the two men older than myself and reminded them of what the general manager had promised us, asking them if they didn't intend to kick for their promotion. At first they said, " Ah, what's the use? The engineer asked for that man; and if we make a fuss, we might get the place, but both the master mechanic and the engineer would be down on us, and it would not do us any good."

I reminded them that eternal vigilance was the price of liberty, asked them what they were firing for, and told them they were fools to allow their rights to be taken from them without a protest. Finally they said that if I would go with them, they would request the master mechanic to do the right thing.

"No, sir," said I; "I'll head no more committees for you fellows; but if you are not going to demand your rights, I am mine. I'll not permit a man to be promoted over my head if I can help it."

I marched directly to the master mechanic's office. He was in, and looking up, as I fancied, rather suspiciously — or shall I say guiltily? — demanded to know my business. I told him that I understood that it was the policy of the road to promote men according to their seniority, and as a younger than I had been promoted, I had come in to see him about it.

"Who is it?" said he.

"Peterson, sir."

"Is Peterson a younger man than you?"

"Yes, sir."

He called for a book, which he looked over, and then said, "Yes, he is; but Whitworth and Collins are both your seniors, so I don't see as you are entitled to anything."

I told him they were the only two ahead of me; but that if he put Peterson ahead, that made three; that I had fired over two years, and didn't see why I should forfeit promotion in favor of another. He closed the book with a bang, asked me if I wanted that train, and when I said I did, he answered, "All right, sir; you can have it."

"Shall I take her next trip, sir?"

"Yes; or you can pay your fare to ——, and fire her back to-night, if you like," savagely.

I thanked him as humbly as I could and went out, my heart somewhat misgiving me. Whitworth and Collins asked me how I made out.

"I got the train," said I.

"Bully for you!" said Whitworth.

"You won't keep it a week," said Collins.

"Well, I've got it, anyway, and I'll keep it as long as I can, and I won't be put off it for nothing, either," said I, my courage returning now that I was clear of the office.

The next day I came down to the round-house bright and early, so as to be sure and have my engine ready on time and in good shape, for I knew I would not be apt to get a very cordial reception from the engineer, and I didn't want to give him cause for complaint. I had her shining like a glass bottle full of pitch when he came along. He was a surly, important fellow, very unpopular with the firemen, as he was one of those who believed that a locomotive engineer was little, if any, lower than the gods, and firemen were especially created to be their servants. When he climbed aboard and saw me busily at work, he stopped short, and said, —

"What are you doin' on this engine?"

"Getting her ready to go out."

"What's the matter with Billy?"

"Nothing as I know of. This train don't belong to him, so he's been put back on freight."

"Oho! so you've worked him out of his job, hey?"

"No, I have got him out of my job, that's all."

"Your job, hey? You can't fire this train."

"How do you know?"

"Because you never fired a passenger train, an' this is an almighty hard train. I got Billy Peterson put on here because I wanted him, an' now you've got his job away from him; by G—d, things are coming to a fine pass when firemen run the road. I'll tell you one thing, my young buck: you've bit off more 'n you can chew this time; if I don't give you a belly-full before you see this round-house again, you can call me a quaker!"

He was a big two hundred and forty pounder, but from his mean, overbearing way, I had long ago judged him to be a coward. I knew that he disliked me especially for the action I had taken in going to the general manager, and I knew, too, that if I let him once begin to bully me, I would have a dog's life as long as I staid with him, so I determined to have it out right then and there.

"See here, Mr. Simpson," said I; "I don't know of any firemen that are running the road, but I do know that no engineers are running it. The day when firemen had no rights on this road is past, and you may as well admit that fact. This train belongs to me. I can fire it as well as anybody; and if you work against me to knock me out, I'll beat you at your own game and get you discharged."

He sat and stared at me, with his mouth open in amazement, while I uttered this pure bluff, then regaining his senses, he jumped down off the engine in a rage, saying, "Well, d—n you, anyhow; I won't take you if I have to go out alone." And off he went to the office, but came back again directly, and without a word pulled out for the train-shed. After we got coupled on, and while waiting for the conductor's signal, he turned to me and said, "You've forced yourself on here where you're not wanted, and now mind what I tell you: you'll keep this engine hot, or I'll do a little reporting to the general manager myself; then we'll see who'll get discharged."

"All right," said I. "I can keep her hot if you run her right; and now let me tell you something: I'm entitled to this job, and I'm going to have it, in spite of you; and if I lose it for any reason, whether it's my fault or not, I'll make no reports to anybody,

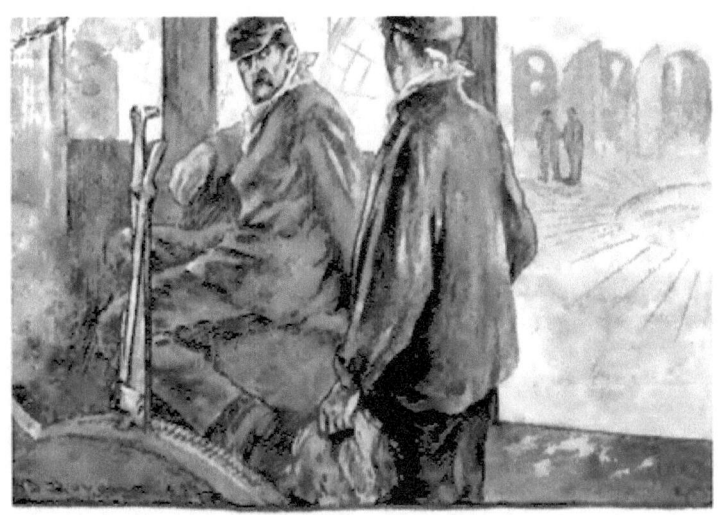

"'You've forced yourself on here where you're not wanted.'" — p. 116.

but I'll lick you every day for a year, as big as you are. And if you have any doubts about my ability to do it, jump right down here on the ground, and I'll give you the first dose before leaving-time."

I heard the conductor call out "All aboard!" saw Simpson look back, and as he jerked the throttle wide open, I rang the bell with one hand, and opened the fire door with the other, keeping it open until he got through slipping her.

Not another word passed between us during the trip. I kept her good and hot. He ran her correctly, and on the return run he told me he didn't blame me any for the stand I had taken, as a man would be a fool not to get what belonged to him on a railroad, if he could.

I fired for him nearly two years; and though I could never quite forget the attitude he had assumed toward me at first, we became eventually quite good friends. He understood his business thoroughly, and could make time easily with a train that would have kept some of the old runners on the anxious seat. He would insist on having his engine kept in first-class repair, even though he had to have a stand-up row with the master mechanic to get the work done, all of which made my work much easier. The natural consequence was that we made a name for fast runs, and were frequently sent out with specials. I paid particular attention to his method of handling her, and thereby gained a thorough knowledge of the most successful manner of handling trains and engines — a knowledge which was afterwards of inestimable value to me.

I have mentioned the fact that railroad superintendents wink at violation of rules sometimes, if thereby good runs are made, *and no harm comes from it*. There was a fast express from the east which seldom arrived on time during the winter, being delayed by snow. As it was an early morning train into Chicago, and of a somewhat local nature on our division, business men were continually complaining of the delay and inconvenience caused them by its being late; so one winter, in order to satisfy them, a first section was run over the division, hauled by the regular engine, to do the local work, and we were stationed with our engine at the other end of the division, to take the regular train when it came along, and run it as a second section, making no stops unless there were passengers to get off, which seldom occurred. It was an open secret that this job was given to Simpson on account of his record breaking proclivities, and the superintendent would usually meet us on the station platform, and congratulate him on his lightning run; for we would frequently make up an hour and a half, following the first section right in. Now, of course, the superintendent knew that in order to make such flying trips as that, it was necessary to disregard yard-limit rules and slow-downs; but he was so pleased with the record the road was making in delivering its eastern train on time, that he said never a word.

Some eighty miles out from Chicago there was a small city, where we had a large freight-yard nearly three miles long. The yard-limit rule required all engines to reduce speed to six miles an hour, when running within the limits of any railroad yard — a rule that was never respected by any one, nor enforced; it was merely a hole for the company to crawl out of in case of a collision in the yard. No train could make time if the engineer observed that rule, for there were miles and miles of yards on the division. It is also a rigid rule that the main track must not be used between sections of a first-class train, for the sections are all regarded as one train, consequently the train has not passed until the last section has gone. Now, while this rule is sometimes violated, and nobody the wiser, "Hell-fire Jack and second four" were so well known by all employees, that nobody would take chances, *as a rule*, of getting between her and her first section for a minute; but on a certain unfortunate morning a freight crew were doing some switching in the yard I speak of, and before they went to work the conductor had learned from the operator that "second four" was an hour and fifteen minutes late; so as it was reasonable to suppose that she would be at least half an hour late at the yard, he instructed his flagman to hold her, unless he was called in before she arrived. This would give him a chance to use that track for a few minutes if he needed it, as he knew that even if the miraculous happened, and second four made up more time than it was in human power to do, he would be protected until he could get off her track, close the switch, and call his flag. In fact, he did the unpardonable in railroading, — he "took chances."

It so happened that after "first four" passed, he had occasion to cross to the other side of the yard; so he told his engineer of the precautions he had taken, and asked him to cross over. The engineer declined, saying he knew better than to cross over between sections of a first-class train. They argued the question awhile, and finally the conductor persuaded him that he would be foolish to lay there half an hour or more waiting for her, when it was only a minute's work to slip across, — and they were protected anyhow. At last, being over-persuaded, the engineer said, "All right; get your switches open, and I'll cross over." During this conversation more minutes than they thought had gone by. Everything having been favorable, we had made a most extraordinary run; and the flagman, knowing that his conductor would not dare hold a first-class train, had not gone out very far, and was listening for the whistle signal which should tell him to let second four come, when we came wheeling round the curve sixty-five miles an hour.

He frantically waved his red flag as we flew by. Jack shut off, reversed, applied the air-brake and blew a blast on his whistle that made that freight crew's hair stand on end. Their engine was squarely out on the track ahead of us, backing over. The engineer pulled his throttle wide open in the effort to get across, but he hadn't time. We hit her right on the back drive; both engines rolled over on their sides, and both engineers and firemen were thrown out of their cabs and rolled around the yard. Luckily no one was seriously injured, though several passengers were bruised and cut by flying glass, and the tracks were pretty well torn up.

While Jack and I were busy getting the fire out of our engine the conductor went up to the telegraph office and reported the wreck, and inside of an hour a new train was backed down on one of the yard tracks, our passengers and baggage transferred, and we went on. Next day all hands were called to the office, and from the mass of lies we told, the superintendent sifted the truth; and the conductor, engineer, and flagman of the freight were discharged at once, and Jack was suspended.

After he had loafed over thirty days, and heard nothing from the superintendent, he called on the gentleman, and asked what he was going to do with him. The superintendent blazed out wrathfully: "I don't know what to do with you. If the law allowed me to, I'd hang you; a man who would go through a yard as you did ought to be hung." To which Jack replied in righteous indignation, "Well, I wish you'd do something with me. I can't afford to lay round here all summer waiting for you to make up your mind."

"You needn't lay round one minute. Do you understand that? Not one minute."

Jack wasn't discharged; he was too good a man to let go, but after he got back to work he said that if they wanted any more records broken they might get somebody else to do it; he was going to run according to the rules.

While on the passenger train I learned to wonder at the temerity with which people get in the way of trains and so get themselves killed; and I noticed that it was almost a universal practice with people driving across the track, when they hear a train coming, and especially if the engineer whistles to them to get off the track, to yank on the lines instead of plying the whip — now I wonder why they do that.

I remember one case of an old fellow driving across the track slowly, and leading a cow behind the wagon. We came on him rather suddenly round a curve, though he must have heard Jack blow for the crossing half a mile back. There he was, square on the track; Jack whistled at him, and I rung the bell. With the rare presence of mind of his class, he commenced to saw viciously on the lines. His old crowbait of a horse shook his head in dumb protest, and settled back in the breeching. It was impossible to check the train. The cow had proceeded far enough so that the point of the pilot passed under her belly, raising her a dozen feet in the air. She turned a half somersault, and fell on her back across the seat alongside of the farmer; but her weight was more than the antediluvian vehicle could stand, so down it went, all of a heap, like the "Wonderful One

Hoss Shay," the farmer himself turning some kind of a flip-flap out over the body of the cow. Looking back, I saw him get up and shake his fist at us, so I told Jack he was all right, and we went on; but I believe the company paid for both his cow and wagon.

One evening, just as the conductor gave the signal, and we had started from the water-plug, the operator came flying out of his office, waving an order and shouting like mad. We were four minutes late, and as I shouted "whoa" to Jack, I could see that he was mad. But that same four minutes was our salvation; for if we had got away from that station on time, we would have met with a very large surprise party a little later. The operator handed up an order to the effect that engine 96 had run away from —— and was coming east on the west-bound track. That was all, and enough, too; we knew she was coming, heading for us, but how far away she was, or how fast she was coming, we didn't know. It was a time to think and act quickly. Right behind us was an iron bridge eighty feet above the rocky bed of a mountain stream; an eighth of a mile beyond the bridge was a cross-over switch. As there was no siding on our track, our only way was to back over this. Although we were tolerably sure that there was nothing coming behind us on our track, still it is a grave violation of the rules to back up without first sending a flag back to protect you. There was nothing else for it, however, so Jack, shouting to the operator to hold everything east bound, as he was going to back over, commenced backing right away, telling me to notify the conductor and get back on the engine as quickly as possible.

When I got back, he told me to watch out ahead, and if I saw her coming, to sing out, so as we could get off if she was coming like hell. It was an anxious moment; the rear brakeman was giving the signal, and when we got near the switch it was necessary to slack up so he could get off, unlock, and open it. I don't suppose that switch had been used much; that was the only time I ever saw it used. And passenger brakemen are proverbially slow at such matters, for they hate to soil their white hands and good clothes. It seemed as if he would never get it over. Jack had to come to a full stop to keep from running over it, and I could hear him muttering curses on the unfortunate brakeman, who, I have no doubt, was doing his level best, and at last got the switch open; then it appeared that the conductor had not had sufficient forethought to send another man to the other one, but the same fellow had to go and fumble with it, calling forth more anathemas from us. At last we got the welcome signal to back up, and he gave her a jerk back that made all the passengers bob their heads. The way we went over those cross-over switches was a flagrant violation of all railroad precedent, but we got across all right, and I jumped off and closed the head switch.

"Now, d—n her, let her come!" said Jack.

It was getting dark. We got off and walked up to the station to find out as many particulars as we could. All the agent knew was that she had passed the first station, eight miles out, in less than seven minutes after it was discovered that she had gone off on her own hook. As she should have passed by some time ago at that rate of going, we judged that she had either slowed up or ditched herself, and Jack and I were arguing the advisability of asking permission to cut our engine loose, and run down on the opposite track in search of her, when a chorus of "Here she comes!" from the crowd of passengers and countrymen who had gathered at the station called our attention to the track.

It was a strange and weird sight that met our gaze. The crowd stood silent and breathless as she passed. She had slowed down to about twenty miles per hour, and as she was hooked up to within one short notch of the centre, the steam had gone down, and her cylinder cocks were open, and there was no perceptible exhaust from the stack, but only a slight phit! phit! from the cylinder cocks as she silently loomed up in the dusk. Big, black, and indistinct she crept up to us, all hands drawing back as though she was something uncanny. Not a sound of whistle or bell heralded her approach; not a glimmer of light showed her the way, but like an apparition she appeared to us for an instant, and was gone; swallowed up in the night so quickly and silently, that we could hardly believe our own eyes.

For an instant we stood like a lot of dummies, looking at the blackness where she had been; then Jack broke the spell by calling to the conductor to cut our engine off and open the switches, saying that as she was so nearly out of steam we could easily catch her and bring her back. So we crossed over and started after her, and this was a ticklish job. As we were backing, our headlight didn't show, while she had no lights at all, and no man could tell where she might stop or leave the track, so it was a case of guess. If we ran too slow, we might chase her for miles, or again we might run into her unexpectedly at any moment, wrecking both tenders.

A brakeman and myself stood on the rear of our tender, holding lanterns aloft, and watching with all our eyes, while the conductor rode in my side of the cab, unconsciously ringing the bell, as if to warn her not to get herself run down. Across the long bridge we went carefully, around the curve, and up a slight grade, and — there she stood, spent, her picnicking done.

I jumped aboard, found that her fire, which had been banked ahead, was nearly out; her steam was down to forty-five pounds, throttle barely open, and reverse lever within a notch of the centre, with no water in her lower gauge cock, although she stood head up the grade. There was no sign of a leak, however, so we coupled them together, and Jack gave her a jerk back and then stopped, whereupon she showed water in the lower gauge, so we knew she hadn't run dry altogether.

We towed her back to the yard, I dumped what remained of her fire, and we went on.

Now what do you suppose caused that engine to run away, endangering not only the first train she might meet (which was ours), but also the lives of all persons and animals that might have had occasion to cross the track while she was sneaking silently up the road?

A weak throttle latch-spring, which had been reported over and over again, and which would have cost to replace probably from three to four cents. Of course it was attended to at once after this most providential escape? Not at all. I ran her a year afterwards with the same flimsy spring, and had a set of blocks to check her wheels, in order to prevent a recurrence of the adventure while she was in my charge.

Why didn't I report it? I did, daily, until I got tired of doing so.

On the evening when she headed us, the hostler had cleaned her fire and backed her down into "the hole"; he was in a hurry,—that was his normal condition. He should have had two helpers, but didn't have any, so he shut her off, pulled the lever up on the centre (approximately) and opened the cylinder cocks, thereby complying with the rules; then he jumped off and went after another engine. The weak spring failed to latch the throttle shut, it worked open a little way, and being light, not yet coaled or watered, she crawled up out of "the hole" in spite of her open cylinder cocks, and started off down the yard. In cleaning the fire a spark had ignited the waste on top of the back driving-box. The blaze attracted the attention of my old friend Pop, who was oiling his engine, and talking with a couple of firemen as she passed. Thinking that the hostler was taking her out to the coal pockets, he shouted, "Hey! yer back drivin'-box is afire." As no one answered, they all looked carefully at her and saw that she was alone. A shout went up, "That engine's runnin' away!" The fireman of a near-by switch engine heard the cry, leaped to the ground and sprinted after her, visions of promotion no doubt flitting before his mind's eye, and luring him to phenomenal bursts of speed. In the meantime old 96, having passed all the switches, and got upon the main track, was gaining speed with every revolution of her big drivers. The fireman touched the back of her tank with the tips of his outstretched fingers, and then with a derisive wiggle of her drawhead she glided away.

He was directly in front of the telegraph office when he realized that the race was lost, and his brief dream of speedy promotion over; with a presence of mind highly commendable, he rushed into the office, told the operator what had happened, and advised him to tell Wilson, eight miles away, to side-track her. Wilson got the message all right, and as he had some little distance to go to the switch, started on the run. As he opened the door, a meteor shot by, and glancing up the line, a faint glimpse of the back end of a tender with a big, yellow 96 on it, disappearing round the curve in a cloud of dust told him she had gone.

Two miles from where she started there was a turnout around a sink-hole. As the company had either to buy land enough from the farmer to build the turnout, or erect an expensive suspension bridge over the hole, he had shrewdly taken advantage of their necessity to charge such a gold-mine price, that they bought what would barely serve their purpose; consequently each end of the turnout was such a dangerously sharp curve that a watchman was stationed there to show a slow-down signal, and report all engineers going over it at a faster speed than six miles an hour. As it was a hard pull across with freight trains, the engineers would slow down a bit until the engine took the entering curve and then pull out; whereupon, "Dinny" would drop his green flag, and brandishing the red, bawl out with true Irish importance, "I'll repoort you for disrispictin' me red signal," and the breeze would waft back the answer to his outraged dignity, "Ah, go to ——"

On this afternoon Dinny saw "some felly comin' like the divil batin' tan-bark." Firm in the resolution to flag him, he jumped to the middle of the track with his red flag; but before he could give it more than one desperate wave, he realized that the best place for him was in a little frog-pond behind his shanty; with one bound he was into it, and his threat to "repoort" was smothered in the thick green slime, as 96, most contemptuously "disrispictin'" the red, flew by.

The fact that the 96 passed over it in safety was such a vivid object lesson to the superintendent that Dinny was removed from his important position where he could sass engineers, and returned to the section gang.

CHAPTER X

A CLAM CHOWDER — PROMOTION — THE TRAIN MASTER'S CONUNDRUMS — AT THE THROTTLE — WRECKING AN ENGINE — DISCHARGED — ANOTHER APPEAL — REINSTATED

THE engineers had a clam chowder. It becomes absolutely necessary sometimes for men whose daily lives are passed under the strictest discipline, and in a calling where their nerves are ever at concert pitch, to unbend, relax the rigid tension, and do things which would appear silly under other circumstances, or even vicious. There is a certain amount of the old Adam in everybody, which it is not wholesome to suppress entirely; and as a railroad man's private life is to a certain extent under the surveillance of his superiors, it does him good to get beyond their ken occasionally, and do just as he pleases, even to the extent perhaps of getting a little drunk, just for the devilment of it.

I guess they had a pretty good time, though all that we outsiders could find out about it was that which was dropped in our hearing, when they reviewed their escapades.

To one poor fellow, however, it was a most serious event, as it finally cost him his life. He was climbing a fruit tree, when one of the others, in the exuberance of his animal spirits, caught up an old piece of board and gave him a mighty slap with it on the part of his anatomy where his trousers fitted tightest. With a yell of rage and pain the victim, amid the uproarious laughter of his comrades, dropped from the tree and chased his tormentor about the place, which, as they were both three-hundred-pound men, and the day was fearfully hot, proved a first-class diversion to the crowd. After evening the matter up with the fellow who hit him, somebody called his attention to the fact that his light trousers were stained with blood. An investigation showed that the piece of board contained a short, rusty nail which had penetrated the skin, but owing to the greater pain caused by the blow, it had not been noticed at the time. Nothing was thought of it, but after making one trip on his engine he laid off lame, and died of blood-poisoning inside of a week.

We had been having very poor coal; nearly all trains were losing some time, and the master mechanic had firemen "on the carpet" daily, jacking them up for a week or ten days on account of their inability to make steam with material which, however suitable for roadbed ballast, was never intended by the Almighty for fuel. Owing to the expert skill of my engineer, I had not yet been put through that ordeal; we had managed to crawl in on time every day, but it was all we could do, an extra car or a hard-hauling train would have surely dumped us.

It was about a week after the funeral of the unfortunate engineer, that we made our first break, and it was a bad one. I couldn't keep her hot to save my soul. Jack favored her, and helped me all he could; but it was no use, she would lag in spite of all I could do. I was ashamed, and mad clean through, for we dropped twenty minutes.

Twenty minutes on the limited, and every minute of it for the want of steam! I foresaw a very interesting interview with the master mechanic when I should get back; my pride was hurt. I had been the only fireman so far who had not "dropped his bundle," and now I had done worse than any of them. I feared that I should be taken off the train altogether; suspended I knew I should be, possibly for thirty days. So it was with a heavy heart that I fired the old engine back, for I knew that excuses, however valid, didn't go with the "old man," his invariable reply to all such being, "That don't make any difference." I believe he would have said that if you had told him that the reason you didn't make time was because you lost all the wheels off the engine, and the way he said it was extremely aggravating; for he was boss, and it would do no good to talk back.

When we got to the round-house, my heart sank as I saw the foreman approaching me, looking grave, as though he didn't half like the errand he was on; for I had always been rather a favorite with him, and an example to be held up to the other firemen.

"The old man wants to see you in the office," said he.

"All right."

And now that my worst fears were confirmed I felt my courage return, and I resolved not to submit to any of his sneering remarks. He could jack me up — that was his privilege; but if he made any disparaging comments, as he usually did in such cases, I vowed to myself that I'd talk United States to him if I lost my job by it; so putting on as bold a front as I could, I stepped over to the office.

He was standing with his back to me, looking out the window when I entered, but turned at once, and said, —

"Well, sir?"

I told him I had been ordered to report to him.

"Oh, yes," said he; "freight is picking up now, and since Mr. Kimball's death we are rather short handed; do you think you can run an engine?"

Heavens and earth, promotion! This was an agreeable surprise, with a vengeance. I knew the stereotyped question, "Do you think you can run an engine?" I had heard so many of the boys tell of it as part of their experience when they were promoted, and I knew, too, the stereotyped answer: "I dunno, sir; I never tried." I had always promised myself that when it came my turn to answer the all-important question I wouldn't say *that* anyhow; so after catching my breath a bit, I answered as bold as brass, "Yes, sir."

"Yes, I have no doubt that you can; I've had my eye on you ever since you came here, and with one or two exceptions your conduct has been very satisfactory."

He then proceeded to examine me on the locomotive: as to how it was constructed, and what I would do in various emergencies, the idea being to show how in case of a breakdown I would temporarily repair my engine, so as to get the train home with as little delay to the traffic of the road as possible; and although he suggested several mishaps, the like of which I had never heard discussed before, I kept my wits about me, and satisfied him that I was to be trusted. He gave me some advice concerning my deportment towards the employees in the other departments of the service, assured me that as long as I was right he would stand by me, — which I am afraid made me open my eyes rather widely, for nobody ever heard of him standing by his men, — and then handing me a note to the train master, told me to go and pass his examination and hurry back, "For," said he, "I shall want you to go out to-night."

The train master tangled me up a little once or twice with his conundrums, and I feared I wasn't making a very good showing in answer to the question, what I would do if, when running a first-class train on a single-track branch, I had orders to meet and pass another first-class train at the junction of the double-track main line, and on arriving there, found that she had not yet arrived.

I answered that I would wait until she did.

"Suppose she was an hour late?"

"That's none of my business."

"What! would you hold those passengers there an hour with a double track ahead of you?"

I wasn't quite sure, but answered desperately, "Certainly, if I had orders to wait there."

He brought down his fist with a bang on the table, and roared out, "That's right; I want you always to remember that when an order is given to you, it's good until fulfilled, and is to be obeyed. I'll run the trains from here — that's what I'm hired for; I won't have conductors and engineers running trains.

"Now suppose you was running a first-class train, and you got a regardless order to run the opposite track to the next station, what would you do when you got there?"

"Cross back again and proceed on my rights."

"What rights?"

"My time-table rights."

"Good agin! By G—, some o' those fellers would wait there twenty-four hours for an order to put 'em on the time table."

He kept this kind of thing up for a good hour, sometimes puzzling me considerably, but on the whole, I didn't make any very bad breaks. At last looking at his watch, he said, "H—l! it's dinner time. You can tell Mr. Seely that I'm satisfied."

At last! I had reached the goal for which I had toiled so long, and so hard; and when I went back, reported to Mr. Seely, and got orders to take engine 80 at 9 P.M., I was the proudest and happiest young fellow in the state.

The position of locomotive engineer is a very peculiar one, calling for widely different qualities. He must be brave to recklessness when the occasion demands it, and yet extremely careful, both of the machine under his control, and as to the handling of his train; for while he will be held strictly accountable for the slightest damage caused either by carelessness or ignorance on his part, there are circumstances under which the company will justify him in wilfully wrecking the machine, to avoid greater damage. As his judgment must be formed instantly, and amid the most exciting surroundings, and afterwards put to the severe test of comparison with some other method which the master mechanic has thought out in the leisure of his cushioned office chair, it can be seen that rare attainments must be possessed by the man on "the head end" if he would hold his job. Nor is this by any means all. He is expected to have and to exercise better judgment than the other employees; and as they have no orders to submit to his will, friction arises, he is d——d for a crank, and when an accident occurs, conductors, brakemen, and switchmen all unite to swear the blame on the unfortunate engineer, who being in the minority, is lucky indeed if he escapes discharge.

As their ranks are recruited mostly from the farmers' boys along the line, with no special aptitude for the business, and who learn it by passing an apprenticeship similar to mine, and as the promoted men get at first the most difficult jobs for a beginner, switching in crowded yards, hauling wildcat freight, and doing all sorts of odd jobs, with the worst old worn-out scrap-heaps of engines in the company's possession, what wonder that so many young runners, whose mishaps are all attributed to their incompetency, are discharged, when if the same accident had happened to an experienced man, but little notice would have been taken, or at least his explanation would have carried *some* weight.

Then, again, the very fact that he is known to be a young runner causes him to be the recipient of an immense amount of worthless advice from everybody, even his own fireman. If he is weak enough to act upon the advice of others, because he thinks they may know better than he does, and gets into trouble, he will find that no one has any sympathy for his case, least of all the super. "You had no business to do it, no matter who advised you to, if you didn't think it was right," he is told.

If, on the other hand, he is stiff, and tells his would-be advisers that he is competent to judge for himself, he makes enemies, so that when the time comes that two heads would be better than one, he is told, "Do as you d—d please; you know it all."

I will illustrate right here what I have said about an engineer being sustained in wilfully damaging his engine. It was the first winter after I was promoted;

there had been a heavy fall of snow, and I was ordered to couple in ahead of a west-bound passenger train, to help the regular engine drag her through the big drifts. I had a brand-new engine right out of the shop. It is desired that a locomotive's driving-wheel tires shall make if possible a hundred thousand miles before they are worn out. They become grooved by the wear on the rails, requiring to be turned off in the lathe twice, and occasionally three times. As this turning-off process is equivalent to many miles of legitimate wear, it is to be avoided as long as possible, and as there is always rivalry between the division master mechanics, the engineer who reduces the life of a set of tires is not to be envied. The division superintendent had the snow-plough out, and as it was working on our track, we got an order to run on the east-bound track to the next station, regardless of all opposing trains, which means that the track is clear for us. The snow-plough crew had a flag out to protect themselves; for although they knew the operator had orders not to let anything come, still you are always supposed to protect yourself. As I was on the head engine, I had all the looking out to do, the other fellow having his windows closed to keep out the snow, so that he could ride along warm and comfortable.

I could hardly see anything myself, for the drifting snow made it impossible to keep one's eyes open with the head out, and if I closed my windows, they instantly became coated with it. I managed to see most of the whistling-posts, however, and if I had any doubts about having passed one, I blew the crossing signal anyway. I told the fireman to keep as good a lookout on his side as possible; for, as the cab and boiler sheltered him, he could at least look out without closing his eyes.

It seems that the flagman heard me blow for a road crossing, and as all the landmarks were obliterated by snow, he was unable to say on which track we were coming, so, to be on the safe side he flagged us anyway; the snow not being so very deep here, we were coming at a pretty good gait, and when he saw that the engines continued to use steam, he realized that the blinding snow made his signal invisible to the engineer, and jumped to the other side of the track, waving his flag frantically, and yelling at the top of his voice. My fireman happening just then to glance ahead, saw his gymnastics, and judging that collision must be imminent, yelled "Whoa!" and jumped off.

As I could see nothing, I shut off, blew "brakes" to the other engineer, applied my own, and then as he had not heard me, and was still using steam, shoving me into I knew not what, I whistled to him again, reversed and gave her sand, he still shoving me ahead as hard as he could.

My driver-brake being set, and engine reversed, the big wheels were held stationary as in a vise, while she skated, grating and grinding along on the sanded rails. I knew I was playing havoc with those new

"We found grooves nearly a quarter of an inch deep." — p. 141.

tires; but what could I do? I expected every instant to have the end of a car come smashing into my cab. Again and again I blew the brake signal; the grade was in our favor, so that my partner was able to keep them going in spite of me, and he shoved the whole business clear by the snow-plough. Her crew hearing my signals, and seeing my wheels locked, managed to attract his attention, and at last we got stopped.

The superintendent climbed into my cab, and asked me if that fellow flagged me. I told him he did, and explained the whole affair. He understood, said, "All right; there's no harm done. Go on." But I told him I believed there had been a good deal of harm done, and explained what I had done.

"Blow 'off brakes' and turn her over," said he, "and let's see how she goes."

I did so, and you would have sworn that she had square wheels. When she came to the "flat spots" she seemed to drop a foot, and come down on the rails like a house falling over; and then when she went over them, she would raise herself bodily again as she came up on to the round surface.

"Holy Moses!" said the superintendent. "Stop, and let's get down and look at these tires."

We found grooves nearly a quarter of an inch deep and six or seven inches long in them. After a little consultation the superintendent ordered us to go on slowly to a junction ten miles ahead, where another engine could be procured to help the train, while I should ask for orders to dead-head home.

"And don't you run this train over six miles an hour," said he, "or you'll break all the rails and knock down all the bridges between here and M——."

I ventured to remark that I supposed I was done.

"What for?" said he, looking at me, in evident surprise.

"For gouging those new ties," said I.

"No, sir; you're not done for that. You got a flag, didn't you?"

"Yes, sir."

"Well, let me tell you one thing. While I'm superintendent of this division, if you ever fail to use every means in your power to stop when you are flagged, I'll discharge you. These engines are to be used in two ways — to haul the trains and to help stop them when necessary. I wouldn't care if you'd tied a hard knot in her, as long as it was done in an effort to stop when flagged. Go on now, an' get out o' here."

My fireman having returned, we started again, and of all the tough riding I ever did, the worst was done on that engine before I got her back to the yard. I used all the spare nuts and bolts that we had on both engines, replacing what she shook out and broke off before we got to M——. Then I gathered up all I could find in the round-house, and the fireman and I got under her and riveted all the bolts down so the nuts couldn't get off, and having received orders to return "wild," we started. It was only thirty miles, but it was the longest and worst ride by all odds that I ever experienced; and I don't believe there are a dozen railroad men in the country that ever went through a similar experience — the antics that she cut up when coupled to the train were not a mark to her actions now.

We tied the bell fast "on the centre." Before we had gone a mile, the sand-box cover left us somewhere, and before we had covered half the distance, the stack and head lamp were both tied fast on the back of the tender. The whistle pipe broke short off in the dome, and before I got the hole plugged with a piece of broomstick, she had blown her steam down to thirty pounds; and as the injector would only work when standing still, I delayed a couple of passenger trains before I was able to start again. The pilot worked loose, stuck its nose into a tie, and crumbled up. It was only under the most favorable circumstances that I dared leave one siding to run for another. Every time she lit on her grooves, the tender would ram the engine so spitefully that I feared she would shake all the coal out of the gangways before we got home, for the fireman was about as badly used up as I was, and hadn't ambition enough to try to keep it back.

We were all night on the road, and when we came pounding and banging into the yard at ten o'clock the next day, a reception committee, composed of the master mechanic and every man in the department under him, who could possibly get there, were awaiting our arrival.

She was a beautiful sight! No stack, no pilot, no head lamp, the wreck of the cab shackling about with every thump like a barrel with only one hoop, the running gear a mass of grease and dirt, the paint, one dome, sand-box, and cab burned off, and we two human wrecks riding her. She was a railroad Flying Dutchman, and only the day before she had been brand new, glorious in gold leaf and brilliant varnish, glittering brass, and Russia iron.

Within ten feet of where I intended to stop, the coupling-pin of the tender broke, and on her next leap ahead she tore loose from safety-chain and fuel-boxes, leaving it behind. I got down the best way I could; for besides being killed, I was starved to death; and telling the round-house fireman he had better get the fire out of her, as the water was rather low in the boiler, I started to look her over, but seeing a broken equalizer, and immediately afterwards a break in the frame, I gave it up, and simply wrote on the slip, "Engine 207 wants to go in the back shop," filed my report, and went home. I stayed home two days, recuperating, and when I returned, I found an order in the engineer's box for me to call at the office and get my time.

I met the master mechanic coming out as I was going in. He didn't even look at me, but I called him by name, and asked why I was discharged. He stopped, looked at me a moment in superlative contempt, and said, —

"I don't know, I'm sure. I don't see how this

"She was a beautiful sight! No stack, no pilot, no head lamp." — p. 144.

company can afford to dispense with the services of such a valuable man as you are."

I said no more to him, but went at once to the superintendent's office. Fortunately, I found him in, and, for a wonder, unoccupied. When I presented myself, he looked up inquiringly, and without a word I laid the bill of my time on his desk. He looked at it, and said, "Well, what's wrong with this? Isn't your account all right?"

"Oho!" thought I, "he sings a different tune from what he did the other day." So I reminded him that he had promised me that I should not be discharged for what I had done.

"I don't know that you are discharged for that," said he, coldly, as he handed me back my bill; "what did Mr. Seely say he discharged you for?"

I told him the answer Mr. Seely had made to my request for information, and he promised to inquire into it, saying that he would be as good as his word, and that I should not be discharged on that account. I asked him when I might expect to hear from him, and he said he couldn't tell, was very busy just now, but as soon as he had time.

I waited in suspense three weeks, and as it would soon be pay-day, I thought I had better find out if I was to sign the pay-roll for the last time or not. So again I called on the gentleman, and he told me, with a surprised look, that he had sanctioned my discharge ten days ago. He said the master mechanic reported that I brought the engine in a total wreck, and absented myself two days without leave, all of which I was obliged to admit; and as he considered that sufficient, I was graciously allowed to depart, with my hopes and aspirations suffering from a severe frost.

As I was walking down the office stairs, I contrasted the superintendent's and master mechanic's manners with those of the general manager. He was all kindness and geniality, seemed to try to make things as pleasant for us as possible, talked to us, and treated us as though we were his equals and personal friends, whereas they seemed always to think we were their worst enemies. All at once I remembered that he had said to us, "Employees shall certainly have the right of appeal."

I had appealed to him once, and got justice; why not try it again? As before, I had all to gain, and nothing to lose, and I would do it. I went to his office at once, and learned that he was out of town, had gone east, and was not expected back for a week or ten days. All right, I could wait; I had always saved part of my wages, so I had no fear of getting "hard up." To be sure, I would be paid off in the meantime, and in accepting my pay would in a certain sense acknowledge my discharge and close the case; but I knew the general manager was all-powerful, and could, if he chose, reopen it at any time.

I didn't idle away the time, however; for I knew it would be better for me to obtain employment elsewhere, if possible; but though I went the rounds of all the roads, I only found two that had the least idea of hiring any engineers, and when they learned that I had not been running a year, and was already discharged, their interest suddenly collapsed like a worn-out boiler tube, so that at the expiration of ten days I found myself still in undisturbed possession of my liberty.

Again I called at the general manager's office, learned that he had returned the day before, passed through the inquisition in the shape of the old gentleman in the outer office, in the course of which he drew from me the fact that I was discharged, and was seeking reinstatement. He asked me what I expected the general manager to do, and volunteered the opinion that *he* didn't see how that gentleman could interfere, as the division superintendent had sanctioned the matter. He got me so out of patience that I was in the very act of giving him a rude answer, when I heard a quick, elastic step coming from the corridor, and turning, faced the general manager himself, — big, breezy, and genial. He saw me at once, came forward with his hand extended, and a hearty "Ah! good-morning, Mr. M——. Fine morning; what can I do for you? Any one to see me, Stillman?" to the secretary.

"No one but this gentleman, sir."

"Very well; come inside, Mr. M——"

As I followed him into his private office, I wondered how in the world he managed to remember my name; he had never seen me but once in his life, and that was nearly three years ago. As I have since acquired the trick myself, it no longer seems marvellous.

After we were seated, I told him as rapidly and clearly as I could the whole story. He listened carefully without once interrupting, and when I had finished, he asked me what I wanted him to do. I was rather nonplussed at that; for I had hoped he would offer to do something himself, so I answered somewhat sheepishly, that I didn't think I ought to be discharged, as I didn't consider myself to blame for what had happened.

"No," said he, "from your standpoint you certainly are not; but I suppose you know the old saying that one story is good until another is told. Not that I doubt your statement for a moment; but you know your conception of the affair is apt to be colored by your interest; it certainly is a very serious matter for an engineer to take out a brand-new engine, and bring her back wrecked; still, it is quite within the bounds of possibility that you are not altogether to blame. I will look over the master mechanic's and superintendent's reports; and if I find that they do not conflict materially with your story, you will hear from me, probably through one or the other of them. Will that be satisfactory?"

Considering that it was all I had hoped to accomplish, I told him that it would indeed; bade him good-bye, and withdrew, hope once more springing in my breast.

Two days later on returning to the boarding-house for dinner, I was informed that the caller had left word that the master mechanic wished to see me in his office, so down I went, wondering what the verdict would be.

"Well, sir," said he when I entered, "have you got rested?"

"Yes, sir."

"Do you think you can manage now to double the division with one engine?"

"Well, yes, sir, except under very extraordinary circumstances."

"Better not have any more extraordinary circumstances for a while; they don't pay. I don't believe you are any richer for the last one, and I know the company isn't. And now a word of advice: when you get in a tight place, and have an engine with a power brake, don't reverse, after setting your brake; or if you think she will hold more with the lever than with the brake, reverse her, and release your brake; when you have done either, you have done all that you can do, and sliding the wheels don't do any good, but just the reverse. I had to load that engine on a flat car, and send her to the central shop. Her frame was broken in three places, all the springs were gone, and boxes and journals totally ruined. I never saw an engine come out of a wreck so completely worn out: you have already cost this company more than the oldest engineer in the employ. You can go out to the round-house, and report yourself ready to go to work now."

The next day, to the unbounded astonishment of all hands, my name was seen on the blackboard "second-out," and whenever I met any of the boys it was, "Hey, I thought you were discharged," or "Say, old man, how did ye do it? Give us a leaf out o' yer book, will ye?" But I kept my own counsel, and to this day I presume that many of them think I was related to the president or some influential stockholder.

CHAPTER XI

BROKE IN TWO — DOWN HILL FOR LIFE OR DEATH — CABOOSE JUMPS A PRECIPICE — A WRECK — RESULT OF A MORNING'S NAP — THE NEW SUPER — GIT OUT O' HERE — A NEGLECTED ARCH

BEING in the freight service, I got into those tight places, and experienced those hair-raising accidents, which are the particular property of freight crews. For the passenger trains run on schedule time; the road is theirs on their time; their engines and cars receive the most careful attention; station agents, switchmen, telegraph operators, track-gangs, and watchmen, and in fact, all employees, know when they are due, and look out for them — for to delay a passenger train for any cause is a serious offence; and then, too, the superintendent is apt to be riding on any train, and each and every employee, no matter how lowly his position, firmly believes that the "super" cannot possibly ride over the road without seeing him and noting just how he is performing his duties, so that the passenger trains are well looked out for, and it is very seldom that anything happens to them.

But the poor fellows on freight,— they are the ones that get all the hard knocks. Obliged to pick their way over the road between trains, they have no rights at all; they must get to their destination as soon as possible, or there is trouble; *but* they must not exceed the regular schedule of freight-train speed, no matter how good a chance they may have to do so, they must not run by slow signals faster than the rules allow, nor through yards, nor go by a passenger train at a station even on the *off* side; and, over and above all things, they must never get themselves, or allow themselves to be put, in such a position that they will have to flag a passenger train even for an instant. Track repair men and drawbridge tenders all commence to work as soon as the passenger train has gone, when along comes a poor fellow on a freight who has been twenty-four hours on the road, and is trying to get home. He has barely time enough to get to the next siding to clear the following passenger train, and here's a red flag.

"What's the matter?"

"Section foreman's got a rail up," or "Drawbridge is open," or "Construction train is ploughing off a load of gravel," or in fact anything; consequently the freight, being unable to go, delays the passenger, the freight engineer is called to the super's office, all his explanations go for naught, and he is lucky if he gets off with a jawing and being told that he had no business there right ahead of a first-class train. And these are by no means a hundredth part of the little pleasantnesses that tend to turn a man's hair gray, and make him wish he had been born a king.

"'Section foreman's got a rail up.'" — p. 152.

You remember that I hinted at a bad case of "broke in two" that happened to me once; happily it was not disastrous in its results but —

There was on our division a mountain, and the track down this mountain was about seven miles long, and at the top was a tunnel half a mile long, opening out on the down-hill side, on a short curve, handy to look back on and see if your train was all together. The road down the mountain was quite crooked, as such places always are, and so steep that to take a train up its entire length without "doubling," was a feat to brag about. Half-way down, and hidden by a curve from both directions, was a station on one side, and a freight house on the other, and nearly all inward-bound trains had cars for the freight house, which compelled them to cross over the outward-bound track to get to the freight-house siding. The switch to this siding was a "head-on" switch to the outward or down-hill track; and as that place came under the "yard-limit" rule, all freight trains were obliged to come in there dead slow, which they did. Consequently conductors had become careless, and were in the habit of leaving this head-on switch open after they went in, so as to be handy to get out again, and the flagman would go barely around the curve, so he could show his flag to any on-coming train, and stop them before they ran through the open switch.

On the day of which I speak, I had a heavy mixed train, among them being four cars of railroad iron just about in the middle, and when my engine plunged into the tunnel I shut her off; for she would roll all too fast after that, and need a few brakes set. It was early on a summer morning, and I knew the crew were apt to be asleep in the caboose, so I called for brakes to wake them up, but it didn't have the desired effect. I looked back as I came out of the tunnel and watched the cars following each other out until about half the train was through, then there came no more. I pulled out at once and blew the "broke in two" signal again and again, all the time watching back for the rear end of my train. They must have parted just on the crest of the mountain, and the rear section must have nearly stopped before it pitched over and concluded to follow us; for I opened out a good train length, and began to think that the crew must have got their end stopped, when they shot out of that tunnel like a comet, the railroad iron in the lead. Again I pulled out for dear life, and blew my signal — not a man was out on the train, and as it all came through, the caboose (a little four-wheeled affair) was flirted off the track by the whip-like motion of the train in straightening out, and flying through the air dropped into a river more than five hundred feet below.

Now I was in a tight box, not a living soul to set a brake on those cars; for the entire crew, head brakeman and all, went down to death in their caboose — a severe penalty indeed for their neglect of duty in going to sleep on the road; but one which thousands of railroad men have paid, and will continue to pay.

I told my fireman to close the firebox door again, and jump if he wanted to, "For," said I, "we shall probably never get to the bottom of this mountain." I knew that the chances were a hundred to one that somebody would be working in the freight-house track at that time of day with the switch open, and in that case I was bound to go in there and wreck the whole outfit, for I couldn't stop any more than a three-year-old child could stop an earthquake. He looked at the fast-flying telegraph poles and didn't dare to jump; so on we went, faster and faster, yet hardly fast enough; the old engine jumped and rolled so that we could hardly hang on to her; the coal was running out of each gangway in a steady stream, the lids of the tank-boxes flew open, and tools and oil-cans marked our trail.

I shall never forget that wild ride down the mountain if I live to be a thousand years old. When she struck a reverse curve about two miles from the tunnel, the fireman was thrown clear through the cab window, and literally torn limb from limb as he came in contact with the ground. I thought she had left the track altogether, for she rolled almost over, hurling me across the cab and back again, as she struck the reverse end of the curve, and came down on her wheels with a crash, that shivered every pane of glass, and loosened every bolt and joint in the cab, until it was like an old basket, and rolled around with every roll of the engine — a new source of danger to me, for if it left her, it must surely take me with it.

I grabbed the whistle cord again as soon as I was able to steady myself enough, and frantically blew the "broke in two" signal, hoping that it would warn any one who might be in the switch, that I was coming and couldn't stop.

I couldn't see ahead very well; for it seemed as if the wind was blowing a hurricane, and behind me I raised such a cloud of dust, that I couldn't even see the rear car of the section I had. So I just hung on desperately, blew my warning signal, and watched the steam-gauge, and as the steam went down I pulled the throttle out a notch at a time, until at length I had her wide open, hooked up within a couple of notches of the centre, and the exhaust sounded like a continuous roar. And now I saw ahead of me a man in the middle of the track, languidly waving a red flag. Yes; it was all over with me now — the freight-house switch was open. Mechanically I again blew the signal; then realizing that I had not more than half a dozen more breaths to draw in this world, a kind of demoniac frenzy seemed to seize me — a desire to do all the damage possible with my dying breath, to annihilate everything from the face of the earth, as it were. Clutching the reverse lever with both hands, I with difficulty unhooked her, and dropped her down a couple of notches, and as fast as she was going before, I felt

"And now I saw ahead of me a man in the middle of the track."—p. 156.

her leap ahead under the impetus of the longer point of cut-off, and a fierce joy surged over me to think what a world-beater my wreck would be.

Looking ahead again, I saw that the flagman had dropped his flag, and was running at a breakneck speed for the switch. For a wonder they hadn't sent out the biggest dunce on the train to flag. He had sense enough on seeing me coming, and hearing my signal, to comprehend the situation, and wit enough to know the only right thing to do, which was more than I had any right to expect.

Once more coward hope rose in my breast. If he could get that switch closed, the absolute certainty of instant death at that point would be over — the chances were about one in a thousand. To spur him on, I again blew what then sounded to me like the despairing death shriek of the iron devil I rode, and to give him every second of time possible, I shut off my throttle, with the immediate result that the cars bumped up against the tender with a shock that nearly threw me over backwards; but I hung on and watched that man eagerly as he flew with all the speed that was in him for that switch. What if he should stub his toe, as men so often do under like circumstances? It would mean death for me before I could close my eyes; and, even then, I remember thinking how fortunate it was for me, that owing to the proverbial laziness of flagmen, he hadn't gone out as far as the rules required, but had stayed near the switch.

I saw him reach it, and stoop down, clutch the handle, and at the first effort fail to lift it out of the notch in which it lies when the switch is open; and then I swept by like a cyclone. He had got the switch closed just in the nick of time, and the rush of wind from the passing train hurled him down a fifty-foot embankment, bruising him and tearing his clothes, but fortunately doing him no serious injury.

What did the company do to reward him for his heroism in preventing a most disastrous wreck? What did they *do?* Let him off with a reprimand for not having been out a proper distance with his flag, and discharged him within thirty days for a repetition of the offence at the same place.

I saw in the siding the engine that I came so near hitting, and the engine and train crew out in the field, staring with blanched faces; one laggard just tumbling over the fence as I whirled by. I heard a crash, and looking back saw that the corner of the head car had rolled over far enough to break off the water-crane that stood alongside the track, resulting in a bad washout, before they could get the water shut off. I breathed much easier now, and it was with a light heart that I pulled up the lever again and gradually opened her out. I was running through a yard where the rules required me to reduce speed to six miles an hour, but a train going sixty-six could not have kept up with me. I now began to almost enjoy my ride, for the relaxation was so great after what I had passed through that it didn't seem as if there was any more danger now.

There was a passenger station at the foot of the mountain, and looking at my watch, I saw that a train was just about due there; so again I began to blow my signal to warn them to look out for themselves, for the station was on my side of the road, so that passengers and baggage had to cross my track. Yes, there she stood as I came in sight — a little three-car local. Again I blew to them to make sure that they understood what was going on, although I could see that the track ahead of me was clear; for the operator at the preceding station, with rare presence of mind, had telegraphed ahead that I was coming "broke in two," and fast as I went the message beat me, and though I couldn't hear it for the infernal roar and clatter, yet I saw, in answer to my own signal, two short puffs of white steam from the engine's whistle, which meant "All right, come along." And come along I did, I have no doubt, to the amazement of those passengers, who certainly never saw a freight train wheeled at that rate before. The agent had a truck-load of baggage ready to take across as soon as I passed, but the suction of the train drew the whole business under the wheels, and it disappeared. He was discharged because the superintendent said he was a d—d fool.

The engineer of the local told me afterwards that all he saw was the front end of the engine, with my face at the window; then there came a big cloud of dust and a roar, followed directly by another roar as the rear section passed him, and that was all he knew about it.

I was now down the mountain, thank Heaven, and on level ground, but the rear section wasn't, and I hadn't the least idea how far it was behind me; so I kept the old girl waltzing as fast as I could — which wasn't very fast, as my steam was down to sixty pounds. I didn't dare get down and look at my fire, for fear of being killed in case the rear section caught me, which was now more imminent than ever; as while I was losing way on the level ground, their speed would hardly be checked at all.

I now began to think seriously of jumping, and if I had, it would probably have been the last of me; for the bank there was a rock fill formed by blasting out the high rock on the other side of the road. I was still going a good thirty-five or forty miles an hour, and besides, I was so shaken up by that terrible ride, and had undergone such a severe mental strain, that I was as weak as a rag, and lame and sore all over.

Suddenly rounding a curve, I saw a man standing by the switch of a long siding, giving me a frantic "go ahead" signal. At that sight my spirits rose about two thousand per cent, for I knew I was saved.

Giving him an answering toot toot, I dropped my reverse lever down in the corner, and pulled her wide open to get as far from the rear section as possible, and give him all the chance I could to throw the switch, and get out of the way.

This siding itself was on a large curve, and I found before I had gone a quarter of its length that it was partly occupied by a number of loaded coal cars. Now here arose another new combination. There was going to be a wreck on that siding, and I might get caught in it yet; for if I didn't get far enough away from the point of collision, some of the cars would be apt to pile over on top of me, and then again if, in my haste to get out of the way, I got to the further switch at just the right time, they might be shoved out, and ram me. You see, it frequently happens on the railroad that you have to think of several things at once, and not be very long about it, either; and the result of my rapid thinking on this occasion was that I had done enough towards saving the company's property for one day, and that now was a good time to look out for myself a bit.

I pulled her over and "plugged" her; but as my steam was low, I concluded she would stop herself quicker shut off, so I shut her off; and while I was waiting for her to slow up enough to give me a chance to jump on the left side, the crash came.

There was a great smashing and grinding and piling up round the curve behind me; but where I was, the cars merely ran together with a great ker-bump and rattling of links and pins, which I could hear continuing on round the curve ahead as the lost motion between the cars was violently taken up. After the noise stopped a bit I started to back up, when, remembering that in all probability the opposite track was blocked by the wreckage, I ran ahead instead to the next station, and notified the agent to hold all trains until further orders.

I then reported to the train-despatcher by wire, and he ordered me to cross over to the other track and run back to the wreck, find out how the tracks were, and report to him from this station, the agent keeping the track open for my return.

The agent, a bright, ambitious young fellow, who is now a division superintendent on the same road, helped me to fire up, and back I went. I found, as I had expected, that both tracks were blocked, the wrecked cars being piled in heaps, mixed and tangled with the railroad iron that had composed part of my train, while coal, flour, agricultural machinery, and all sorts of merchandise were scattered all over the ground.

All this property and four human lives were lost because the train crew took an early morning nap.

Yes indeed; it is true that if everybody obeyed orders and attended to business, the only accidents on railroads would be those caused by forces over which the company has no control, such as washouts, landslides, and so forth. I know it is claimed that watchmen should be stationed at places where these things are liable to occur, and as a rule this is done; but the trouble is that they often happen where nobody ever had the least idea that there was any danger, and while the watchman is guarding the place that is supposed to be shaky, down comes the whole side of a mountain, or out goes a thousand yards of track, where no one had thought such a thing possible. Then, again, the time of sliding is not given in the time table. Those things are just as likely to happen when a train is passing, or too close to stop, as at any other time.

There was another long hill going the other way, not as long as the last one I spoke of, but much steeper; and near the foot of this hill there was a bridge, which was a curve in itself, and as it was built over a muck-hole, on piles, there were very strict orders for all trains to go over it "dead slow." As the grade, however, continued slightly for half a mile or so beyond the bridge, it was customary for freight trains to roll down the hill about as fast as they dared to hit the bridge, and as soon as the engine was over, to let off all brakes, when the engineer would give her a little steam, and with the momentum acquired on the grade, the train would go flying, which was a great help; and as it was what railroad men call "good running ground," it was considered perfectly safe to do so. One side of the track there was a high rock cut, and on the other a river. This rock cut was frequently inspected by the section gang, and any loose stones that could be pried out were taken down. Nothing had ever fallen there, and nobody expected that anything ever would.

There was a watchman stationed at the bridge to report anybody going over it too fast, and about a mile and a half beyond the foot of the hill, where a tree had once fallen down, bringing a lot of dirt and stones with it, another.

We had a new superintendent, and he was doing a great deal of riding on engines to get points, learn the road, and see whom he could catch violating any of the rules. Well, this night when I climbed up after oiling at the water-plug, I saw somebody sitting on the box on my side; and shoving the torch in his face, discovered the new super. I bid him good evening, called the flag, and went on.

I tried to get him into conversation, but he wasn't at all sociable, so I stuck my head out of the window, and as I rode along I wondered how he came to be at that water-plug, and wished he had got on to ride with somebody else instead of me. It was absolutely necessary to let the conductor know he was there, for at the rate we were in the habit of going down "Hickory Hill" he would be sure to jack us all up for thirty days. But how to do it was the question. I knew he was foxy, and would be sure to get on to any tricks by which I might try to communicate with the caboose. But for once kind fortune favored me, and a slight accident which at any other time would have been very annoying, now helped me out.

In cleaning the fire at the water-plug, a spark had got into the back driving-box, and the fumes of burning waste and oil began to smell quite strong.

Turning to the "headman," I said, "Jimmy, run back in the caboose, and get Clayton's dope-bucket;

I've got a driving-box afire. Hurry up, now; we're getting close to Hickory Hill."

"All right," said Jimmy; and away he went like a lamplighter over the top of the cars. He was a bright boy, and could see as far through a stone wall as the next one, and so could the super; for, turning to me, he said, —

"Isn't it customary to carry dope-buckets on the engines?"

I told him it was, but that the master mechanic had ordered them all off about a month before, which was true.

"Are you going to pack that box before you get to the foot of Hickory?" said he.

"No, sir; but I will be all ready to run into Mill Creek siding when I get down, if I have it on the engine."

"Ah!" said he; "I see," with a sneer, which told me that he did indeed *see* through my little subterfuge.

Well, of course the conductor overdid the thing, and held me up that night down Hickory so that you might have got off anywhere, and picked a hat-full of huckleberries and got on again. I was ashamed myself, the thing was so plain.

When the train had crawled about half-way over the bridge, the super said to me, —

"You'd better blow 'off brakes'; I'd like to get home by bedtime to-morrow, if possible."

So I blew them off, and when I thought the caboose

was over the bridge, and not till then, I hooked her up and pulled out, making up my mind to give him a ride the rest of the way down anyhow.

It was a fine moonlight night, and I soon had the train bobbing along like a string of corks on the edge of a seine. The old girl was doing herself proud, and I said to myself, —

"I'll bet he'll get enough of riding on the hard cover of that box before I get to the siding" — when all at once I saw in the bright moonlight not three telegraph poles away, and square across the track, a rock as big as a small house. I shut her off, yelled "Git out o' here!" and made a scrambling jump over the legs of the super, who was watching the fireman poke the fire.

The next thing I knew I was on the ground, rolling over and over, spreading out my arms and legs trying to stop myself. Before I got stopped, the engine hit the rock, reared partly up, and then turning over, crossed the other track and plunged into the river. Her tank lay on the bank alongside of her, bottom up; three cars leaped clean over her and sank in the deep water; four more climbed over the rock and distributed themselves on the other side of it, tearing up the track and knocking down the telegraph poles.

There had been two flat cars near the middle of the train, loaded with small portable boilers, about ten feet long by three in diameter, and when I got slowed up enough to see anything, the first that caught my eye was one of those boilers rolling after me. Then

I wished I could increase my speed again; but that was out of the question, and even if I had stopped right there, it would have been over me before I could get up, rolling me as flat as a pancake.

For, I suppose, about a minute I was as badly scared as I ever have been in my life; but at last, just as I had about made up my mind to shut my eyes for the last time, one end of the boiler struck against something that turned it from its course, and it rolled into the river. After a few more involuntary revolutions on my part, I also stopped.

During all this time you are to understand that the cars had been climbing on top of the rock and of each other, like a lot of rats trying to escape from a terrier, and had become pretty thoroughly wrecked. We gathered around, and called to each other until all were present except Mr. Gleason, the superintendent, and we then commenced to search the wreck for him. It was difficult hunting, because the cars were piled on top of each other; and though the moon was shining brightly, we should have been better off for a few lanterns, as in among the wreckage, where we expected to find the body, it was, of course, quite dark. Having sent a flag out each way, we were only four to search, and I can say for myself that I could not bring myself to feel with my hands where I was unable to see.

After a while we abandoned the search, until we could get lamps; and as the man who went back had been ordered to flag all the way to the last station and report the wreck to the train-despatcher, we stood idly talking the matter over near the tender, when the conductor suddenly said,—

"Be quiet, boys! I thought I heard something under the tank." We listened a moment, and were sure we heard faint sounds, like something moving and muttering under there.

I ran round to the other side, where I had noticed that one corner was a little raised up, and stooping down called out, "Mr. Gleason!" No answer, but still there was no doubt that somebody or something was under there; so telling the others that I would find out, I crawled in. There had been about half a tank of fine, soft coal in the tender when she turned over, and the tank itself was nearly full of water; so the whole mass was now lying there, a pool of inky black mud; for there was a slight hollow in the ground that just held it nicely.

As I crawled into the mess on my hands and knees, I suddenly bumped heads with some one who immediately drew back.

"Is that you, Mr. Gleason?" said I; but I got no answer, and reaching round in the dark, I soon felt the fur collar of his overcoat, and knew it was he. "If you'll follow me, sir, I'll show you the way out," said I.

We were both on our knees under the tank, and half-way to our waists in the black mud. Without saying a word, he threw his arms about my neck and tried to throw me; but I was a young fellow then and pretty muscular, and realizing that he had gone temporarily crazy, I shouted to the others to come in and help me, while I exerted myself to the utmost to prevent him from throwing me, and at the same time to work him along towards the opening.

And, oh my, what a tussle that was! I can't think of it even yet without half shuddering and half laughing.

After I had called to the fellows outside, not a word was spoken by either of us, — we hadn't the wind to spare. He was a wiry chap, and he was bound not to be taken out; and before the others got inside, by an unlucky slip of my knee, I fell, so that he could get his weight on my neck, and he pressed my face down into the water.

I could hear the conductor calling me by name and asking where I was, and of course was unable to answer or even breathe; but he could hear the hard breathing of the super, and knew pretty near what was the matter. So he hurried as much as he could under the circumstances, and soon had him off of me; and not any too soon, either, for I was nearly suffocated.

With plenty of help, we soon got him out; and I wish you could have seen him when we stood him up in the moonlight!

He was always a very dressy man, and when I found him on the engine that night, if I hadn't known him, I should have thought he was some broker or merchant; for he had on a splendid overcoat with heavy fur collar and cuffs, and, under that, a handsome suit of clothes.

Of course the entire outfit was ruined; and he was a sight for gods and men,— as black as the coal, and as wet as a drowned rat, while he could hardly stand up with the weight of his wet clothes.

His senses returned, though, as soon as he got out into the moonlight, and he asked at once what we had done to protect the road; and, finding we had done all that could be done, he told us his experience. He said that when I jumped past him in the cab, his first thought was that we were about to collide with the rear of a preceding train; but, before he could make a move to get out of the way, he was under the tender, and all recollection of where he was or of what had happened left him at once, and he thought he was in the freight yard on the road he had left. It seems they had been troubled a great deal with freight-yard thieves, and he thought it was a dark, rainy night, and he had gone out to do a little detecting on his own hook. Hearing us talking alongside the tender, and thinking he had found the thieves, he started in our direction, and, as he supposed, stepped into a mud-hole between the tracks. Then when I grappled with him, he thought, of course, that the Philistines had executed a flank movement and collared him.

From the fact, however, that he had no knowledge of the half-hour that elapsed between the overturning of the tank and the time that he heard our voices, it is quite plain that he had been unconscious.

Now that, you see, was a case of a rock-slide in a place that was considered perfectly safe; whereas, at the place a little farther along, where it was considered necessary to keep a watchman day and night, nothing ever happened again as long as I remained on the road, which was several years afterwards.

There was a tunnel on the road under a low hill. It was rock for nearly its whole length, but within a hundred yards of one end they found a kind of loose sand and smooth, round stones, such as you find on the sea-beach; and here it had been necessary to arch the tunnel with brick. In the course of years it was observed that the brick arch showed signs of weakness. The roadmaster reported it, and a bulletin order was issued for all trains to go through that tunnel at a speed not exceeding six miles per hour.

Watchmen were stationed at each end to see that the order was obeyed, and another man was stationed at the bad place to watch it and give timely warning if it showed signs of getting any worse, while presumably the civil engineers of the road were making their plans to repair it without interfering with the traffic, — for that's the way all work has to be done on railroads.

The old arch didn't get any worse, apparently, until one night the "cannon ball" came along, and, agreeably to the bulletin order, the engineer let her roll slowly through the tunnel.

Just as he passed the watchman, one brick dropped from directly over the centre of the track, and, striking the point of the pilot, glanced over and broke against the wall within a foot of the watchman's head, who, luckily, was a rather nervous man, so he ran, yelling for dear life, out of the tunnel, and that saved him.

The engineer instinctively pulled his reverse lever over and applied the brake; then, hearing the bricks clattering down on top of his cab, he let the brake off again, dropped the lever ahead, and gave her steam to get out before the whole roof fell in; and it was just those semi-unconscious acts of his that prevented any loss of life in that case, for next to the engine was an express car, and next to that a baggage car.

The express messenger had just gone to the head end of his car, where his desk was, to look over his way-bills, and the baggage-master had gone back in the smoker to get a drink of water, when down came hundreds of tons of loose sand and stones directly between the two cars, crushing them and burying them so that only the extreme end of each was outside the pile of dirt that filled the tunnel solid full.

The engine broke loose and ran on out of the tunnel altogether; and, after waiting and listening awhile to see if any more was coming down, the fireman and the two watchmen went back with torches and lanterns to see how things looked.

When they got back, they could hear the express

messenger kicking and pounding in the corner of the car, so the fireman returned to the engine, got the axe, and chopped him out.

In the meantime, the frightened passengers made their way back to the next station in the rear, and reported the accident to the station agent, who passed the word along to the superintendent that the engine, baggage, and express cars were buried in the tunnel. The engineer's wife, who was in delicate health, was thrown into convulsions on hearing the report, and died before it was known that her husband had escaped.

CHAPTER XII

OVERWORK — TRUSTING A CONDUCTOR — FIFTY-TWO HOURS ON DUTY — THE CALLER — A TRAMP'S STORY — LEARNING A LESSON — DEATH OF THE TRAMP

OUR lives were not, as you may have been led to suppose, all made up of accidents, by any means. They were varied by long spells of semi-idleness when freight was slack, or being worked to death when it was running heavy, for at such times it is not admitted that men need rest or sleep; and I have had a round-house foreman indignantly ask, "What's the matter with you, that you register for rest? You've only been at work twenty-four hours! There's Tom Bailey has been on his engine thirty-six hours, and he ain't asking for rest yet. Some of you fellows ought to get a job clerkin' in a drug store."

You have probably seen accounts of the inquests on railroad wrecks, where men have testified that they were so worn out with overwork that they were unable to properly attend to business. This is a common occurrence. The worst case of the kind that ever happened to me was when on one occasion, on arriving at the end of the division, after a particularly tedious trip, I was ordered to return at once sixty miles down the road to bring up thirty cars of coal, as fuel for the engines. "And hurry up with it; we want it." I protested that I was tired, and unfit to go, but was told there was nobody else; so I coaled, watered, and oiled up, got the caboose, and started.

It might be thought that after having hauled a heavy train over the road, it would be a snap to go back with nothing but the caboose; whereas, though it is true that better time can be made, yet it is terribly hard riding on a heavy freight engine, with no train to hold her down. She shakes you up like a die in a box, with a peculiar sidewise motion that affects the loins and back, so that before I got half way to where I was going, my back ached like a hollow tooth. However, I was anxious to get there as soon as possible, in order to get back and get some sleep, so I ran her right up to the speed limit, — and a little more, — regardless of my lame back.

When I got there, I found four hours' switching (for which you don't get paid) to get my train together; but at last we got started. One of the important things for an engineer to do is to figure out at what plugs he can take water most advantageously; for as this is a job that causes considerable delay, it is desirable to do as little of it as possible; yet it is a high crime to run out of water, so that lots of brain-fag and worriment are expended on this item. On my trip back I had the hill to climb that we rolled down so slowly the night the super was aboard. No one had ever taken thirty cars of coal up that hill, but I didn't know that; for if I had, I would have allowed for the contingency of doubling the hill, both in my water calculation and in estimating my time ahead of the passenger trains. I knew, of course, that it would be a hard tug up there, so I cautioned the fireman to get a good welding heat on her. I got as much water into her as she would stand, and after oiling the cylinders, took a run for the hill.

We had just taken the hill nicely when the conductor came running over the train, waving his hat and yelling for me to stop. Not knowing what might be the matter, I shut off; when he came up and said he had a hot box on the last car. Perhaps I didn't read the riot act to that conductor, to stop me right at the foot of the hill for a hot box, when, if he knew anything, he knew that long before I could get up there he would be able to walk alongside the car and pack it.

The damage was done though, so I told him to cut the train in two, and I would take my end up while he packed his box. By the time I got my train together again on top of the hill, I had barely water enough to reach the next plug, the fire was in bad shape, and not so very many miles behind us there was a mail train; so the situation resolved itself into this, that with barely water and time enough, and a poor fire, I needed to make an extra good run of fifteen miles. I was far from happy, especially as I could see the steam dropping with the regularity of clock-work, though the fireman was working like a slave. About half-way to where I had to go was a little station, with a crossover switch, and a slight grade against me. I humored her all I could to get over that little lump, for then my immediate troubles would be about over. It was not to be, however; she gave one expiring gasp and died before reaching the summit.

The thing to do now was to back across out of the way of the mail which was nearly due, but there was also a train due on the other track; and as their time of passing this station was only about five minutes apart, the conductor, in obedience to the rule made for just exactly such emergencies, went into the telegraph office to find out if either of the trains were late; for if one was late, we might take advantage of that fact to avoid delaying them both.

They were both on time, and while he was telegraphing both ways to ascertain that fact, the mail came up behind us and stopped.

In a big hurry now, the switches were opened and I was signalled back. As it was slightly down grade, I merely gave them a little kick, and away they rolled. As I went past the conductor, I asked him if he had a man on the rear car to set a brake and stop them after I got across. He said yes; but he lied, and I thought so at the time.

When the engine was over all clear, I called for brakes, but I got no brakes; and they were rolling faster than ever, and in the meantime the other passenger train had arrived and stood facing me. It was now dark, so that all I could see was lamp signals; again and again I called for brakes, but there was no one on the train to set them; the mail had gone, and I ought now to be crossing back again out of the other fellow's way. If I stopped them with the engine, the chances were ninety-nine to a hundred that I should break them in two. It was the only thing to do, though, so as gently as I could I checked them, and, as I fondly hoped, pulled my whole train across out of the way; but, alas! the caboose and two cars had broken off and rolled away down the grade, no one could say how far, so I had to back up again, clear of the switch, cut off the engine, and go back after those cars. There was nobody on them, and the caboose lights had not been lit — consequently it was a hunt in the dark; and as one of the things you mustn't do is to run into and wreck your rear end, when going back after it, I had to go very carefully, while all this time the passenger train stood there waiting. At last I got them, pulled them across in a hurry, although, to be sure, it was hardly worth while to hurry now, and after the passenger train had gone, I shoved them back over the switch again, pulled up the train, shoved it over and coupled them all together, and pulled them back on to my track again.

I was now nearly out of water, and in less than an hour the limited would be on top of us. The next water-plug was five miles away; I cut the engine loose and ran for it, took half a tank as quickly as possible, and started back after my train. In all cases where an engine has to come back after a train in the night, the rules require a man to be stationed on the head car with a lamp to signal the engineer back; but I had no faith in my conductor, so I didn't dare to come back very fast, imagining every minute that I saw the head of the car looming out suddenly from the blackness right behind the tender, and all this time the precious minutes were slipping away — minutes that I needed so badly to get out of the way of the limited.

I was right in not trusting the conductor; for though I came back whistling for a signal, the first thing I saw was the station lights. They were all in there having a smoke — "didn't expect me back so soon," they said.

Though I tried my best to stop, knowing I must be close to the train, I hit it hard enough to break the draw-bar in the car, and by the time they got that fixed up there was no earthly hope of getting to the next siding ahead of the limited, so once more I backed over that crossover, but not until I saw a man swinging a lantern on the last car.

After the limited got by, we pulled across once more, and by this time it was doubtful if I had water enough to get to the siding; but as we had all night before us now, I let her take it easy, and got there after a while, with the tank dry and the boiler not much better. I got down to oil while the fireman was taking water, and discovered that the link-lifting spring was broken, and while I was looking at it and wondering how that could have happened without my knowing it, the head brakeman came up with an order for me to weigh that coal.

My back was almost broken, and I was more than half dead with fatigue and worry, and now I had to weigh thirty cars of coal without a lifting spring. The big cast-iron links and long eccentric rods must have weighed at least two hundred pounds, and as it is necessary in putting cars on the scale to move the engine back and forth continually, I saw what a nice time I was going to have handling that old reverse lever.

There was a way freight engine lying in a spur back of the station, so I telegraphed to the train-despatcher, telling him how I was fixed, and asking permission to use that engine to weigh the coal with. The answer I got was short, but not sweet: "Use the engine you have." Back I went to the yard, and weighed that coal. In order to back her, I had to brace both feet against the front of the cab, and pulling with all my might raise the heavy links; then, perhaps, I would have the misfortune to move the cars half an inch too far, so I would get a signal to go ahead a bit, and on unhooking the lever it would fly forward with such force as nearly to jerk me through the front windows. Remember I was nearly dead with fatigue and hunger, when I started on this most delectable trip. However, if you will work for a corporation, you must do as you're told, and do it when and how you're told, too.

I got the coal weighed, sometime and somehow, coupled on to them, and the conductor coming ahead, began to tell how far we could go if we hurried up, and got out ahead of train 12; but I cut him short by telling him to go in the office and tell Chicago that I couldn't go another foot, until I got five or six hours' sleep. Off he went grumbling that we'd never git anywhere that way. But I knew I should be unable to keep awake, while he could lean back in his caboose and snooze all the way in. Back he came in a few minutes.

"Chicago says, 'All right. Go to sleep.'"

I pulled them into a convenient siding, picked as smooth a lump of coal as I could find in the tender, upholstered it with waste, and spreading my coat on the foot-board for a mattress, dropped the curtain, and curled myself in the short, inconvenient, hot, and dirty cab for a few hours' rest (?) to the tune of the fireman's grumbling. He was the toughest man I ever saw on a railroad or anywhere else. He didn't get fat on hard work — there was no more flesh on him than there is on a bird-cage; but he could stand more grief than the old engine herself, and thrive on it, too. He had been right with me ever since we left Chicago, the day before, shovelling fine feed into the old kettle, — and she had an appetite like a stone-crusher, — yet now he kicked because I wanted rest. He said we might better go on in; it was only two or three hours' run, and then we could get proper rest and a good sleep. He couldn't sleep on an engine, and so he kept his clack going until I begged him to be quiet and let me sleep anyway. With that he got off, and I was in hopes he had gone back to the caboose.

My back ached so, I was so tired, and my position was so cramped and uncomfortable, that it was some time before I could even doze. Just as I began to drop off, I heard some one step up in the tank, and glancing through a hole in the curtain saw that it was the fireman returning, and as he had a cigar in his mouth, I knew he must have been in some gin-mill, as no other place would be open at that time of night. With ponderous caution he approached my side of the engine, making a clattering stumble over the fire-hook, which he had left under foot, and raising the corner of the curtain, peeped cautiously in.

Not caring to be entertained by his idle talk, I breathed heavily as though sound asleep, although it was an effort to take long breaths of the distillery perfume which he wafted into my ill-ventilated chamber. However, I felt that I was suffering in a good cause, as I believed that if left to himself he must eventually go to sleep.

Not he; he stood in the tender, looking around awhile, and scratching himself, then he carefully picked up the hook, and laid it with a clink on top of the tank, opened both the oil and tool boxes and looked into them vacantly for a while, shut each of them with *some* noise, just enough to be irritating, and got down.

"Thank the Lord," thought I, "he's gone to get another drink, and maybe he'll stay till morning."

Not at all. I soon heard a peculiar hissing, grating sound, that told me he was pulling the flue-rod out from the tank-truck bolsters, where he always carried it. So the flues were to be bored! I knew that would put the everlasting veto to my hopes of getting any sleep that night; and though I might have forbidden him doing it, I was so astonished at this display of endurance on his part that I was really ashamed to say a word.

He went at his job with the most elaborate precautions against making noise, but only succeeded in making more, if anything. I lay there and watched him through the hole in the curtain, his face shining with perspiration in spots where he had wiped off the coal dust, as he squatted in the coal and peered into the furnace, ramming, twisting, partly withdrawing and then savagely thrusting in the old flue-rod. Listening to the monotonous scrape of the rod across the bottom of the door, at last I dozed off, as it seemed for about a minute.

Somebody was shaking my shoulder and saying, "Hey! hey!" I looked up, dazed and wondering, into the fireman's grimy face. "Seven's just gone, an' if we foller her, we c'n go right in," said he. "I've got the flues all punched out, an' a good fire; hurry up."

With great difficulty I extricated myself from the reverse lever and seat box, and crawled painfully to my feet. I couldn't realize at first where I was or what was going on. It was just getting daylight, a lovely morning, and as I looked about the yard, trying to locate myself, my eyes fell on the coal train, and memory returned with a rush.

I asked the fireman what it was he had said to me; he repeated it, and I answered sleepily, "All right."

Seven was the midnight train out of Chicago, and if she had gone, there would certainly be ample time for us to get in before the first morning train arrived. I was too dead to look at my watch, so I took the fireman's word for it, whistled for the switch two or three times, and as nobody showed up, I gave her a little steam to stretch the train out, and then reversing, gave her an everlasting set-back on them, at the same time calling for the switch. I did this three times before the fireman, who was watching back on his side, said that somebody was coming. Up came the conductor, mad as a hornet, wanted to know what in h— I was trying to do. "Trying to wake you up so we can get out of here. You was in a terrible pucker to go last night when I wasn't able to, but now I'm ready."

"Well, you needn't smash everything all to pieces, jest cause you're ready! The first time you set back on 'em you upsot the stove, an' all the pipe an' fire was rollin' round in the caboose, an' then while we was tryin' to pick it up an' git the fire out, you come back twice more, an' broke all our dishes an' sot a lot of our clo'es afire. I don't see nothin' so almighty smart about that — are ye ready ter go?"

"Yes, yes! get that gate open and let us out; have ye got a flag out?"

"I'll tend ter the flag." And so, grumbling about the damage in his caboose, he opened the switch, and we were soon jouncing along at a fairly good gait. I was still sleepy and dead; had to keep my head out in the sharp morning air to keep awake at all. Arrived at a water-station about half-way, I told the fireman he had better fill the tank, as there could hardly be enough in it to take us through. While I was oiling, the conductor came up and asked if I was going to sidetrack there. I looked at him a full minute before I could get it through my head what he was driving at. Then I told him, "No, certainly not; why should I sidetrack here?"

"How fur ye goin' fer seven?"

"All the way."

"What time's she due here?"

"Fifty-seven."

"What time ye got now!"

I looked at my watch; it was forty-eight. I asked the conductor if we were clear of the switch.

"Yes."

"Have you got it open?"

"Yes."

"Well, gimme a signal."

I jumped on the engine, and with the conductor

giving a back-up signal, I jolted those cars into the siding fully as fast as it is safe to back over a frog, and called the flag just in time to prevent seven's engineer from getting a sight of it, though he saw the man, and told me afterwards that he "guessed" I hadn't been in the switch "more 'n a week."

Then the fireman and I had a little argument as to what it was that he saw when he thought seven had passed us in the yard. As I was now fairly well awake, I was able to figure the time back, and the only passenger train on the road at that time was one going the other way. After I had proved it by the time table, so that there was no doubt about it, he finally admitted that "By gum, he guessed mebbe I was right." While he had been boring the flues, he had also been figuring in his mind as to what would be the best time for us to leave, and decided that if we followed seven we would be all right, which was perfectly correct; then, with his mind full of seven, he got down to put away his flue-rod, and hearing a train go by, thought, of course, it must be seven. This incident taught me never to take anybody's word for anything that I could verify for myself.

"Well," said I, "we've only got about twenty miles farther to go, and I do hope we'll live to land this train in the yard — I've been with it so long that I take a kind of fatherly interest in it."

It would seem as if that most unlovable damsel, "Misfortune," had at last tired of worrying us; for after seven got away, we proceeded to our destination without further mishap, shoved the train away, and gave up the engine to the hostler. Having been fifty-two hours on her without rest (for the short spell of comparative quiet in the yard could not be so termed), I entered on the register this request, "Have been fifty-two hours on duty. Do not call me until I have had eight hours' sleep, — 9.30 A.M." I then crawled slowly and painfully over to the hotel and went to bed.

I was so completely fagged out, that it was some little time before my aching back would allow me to sleep. I had just dropped off when I was rudely shaken by the caller, and saluted with "Hey! hey! are ye awake now? Come, I've been callin' ye for ten minutes; you're wanted for a stock train. Hurry up now; your engine is all ready; train's standing on main track waiting fer ye." When I got my wits collected so as to realize who I was, and who he was, and what he was talking about, I asked him the time. "Ten-fifteen."

"What! have I only been forty-five minutes off of that engine?"

"That's all."

Without another word I tumbled back on the pillow and pulled the bedclothes over my head, but he understood his business; he had been calling unwilling railroaders for four years, and wouldn't be denied. For a while he shook, and pleaded with me, and then realizing the seriousness of the case, he snatched off the bedclothes. That was the last straw.

I jumped out of bed and made a dive for him; but he had often seen that done before, and was outside the door before I could reach him, and with a parting shot through the crack of the door, "Hurry up now; they're waitin' fer ye," he left.

I gathered up my bedclothes and again crawled uncomfortably into bed, the clothes somehow resolving themselves into inconvenient knots and lumps; whereby my extremities and certain prominent parts of my anatomy were exposed to the disagreeable temperature of the contract-built, *well-ventilated* hotel bedroom; but I was too sleepy and inert to attempt to straighten out the tangle, so I lay and shivered miserably, while a more or less well-defined idea oozed through my soggy brain, that I hadn't seen the last of that caller, for he had a reputation which he had built up under most discouraging circumstances in a difficult business.

Sure enough; just as I was beginning to get my ideas into a pleasant state of haziness once more, the door was fired open with a bang, an Indian yell greeted my outraged sense of hearing, and rolling over, I beheld the exultant countenance of mine enemy, safely outside the door this time, and holding up for my inspection a sheet of dirty yellow colored paper, which I knew was a telegraph form. "Read that now, an' see if ye'll get up or not."

I took the paper and read: "Engineer M——, don't you delay this stock train. W. S. B."

A combined order and threat from the train-despatcher signed with the division superintendent's initials, which are always used by the despatcher on duty, — a peremptory order, to be unquestioningly obeyed. I borrowed the caller's pencil and wrote underneath the order: "W. S. B., — I have been fifty-two hours on duty, am unfit to take stock train or any other train. J. B. M." I handed it to the caller, and telling him that if he disturbed me again for any reason, even though the house should be afire, I would brain him, I once more retired; and although I had no doubt that I had signed my death-warrant, I slept the sleep of the utterly weary.

In answer to the expected letter, I called on the superintendent when I returned, and got my medicine, — thirty days suspension for refusing to obey an order. I was lucky to get off so. He told me that all that saved my job was the fact that an engine came in off the branch opportunely and brought the stock train through. The fact that I was physically incapacitated did not justify me in the least in refusing that order *with his initials attached.* I have always had an idea, however, that my troublesome habit of appealing to the general manager had as much to do with preventing my discharge as the arrival of the engine off the branch.

It was while I was hauling freight that the advance guard of that countless horde of tramps who now infest the country made their appearance on our road. I shall never forget the first one that I saw; for his personality has always remained in my memory as the Moses who was leading the march of the hungry tatterdemalions of the east to the promised land of the great, indefinite "west."

It was a fine, moonlight night, and I had left the other end of the division with a heavy train. Five miles out there was a steep though short grade that we considered ourselves lucky to surmount without "doubling"; but as I had managed to get a little work done on my engine last trip, — boiler washed, leaky tubes rolled out, etc., — she was steaming finely, and she walked that train up the grade, slowly, to be sure, but gallantly for all that. Just as she pitched over the brow of the hill and began to gather headway a bit, I fancied I saw something move, out on the front end. At first I attributed it to the moving of a shadow in the bright moonlight and the gentle rolling and pitching of the engine; but as I naturally kept my eye on it, I presently saw a human foot rise for an instant into the bright, yellow moonlight and drop again out of sight behind the steam-chest.

Disquieting visions of a mangled body on my front end, — that I had "picked up," somewhere, some unfortunate gasping his life out in semi-consciousness, or, worse yet, a badly but not fatally injured person struggling, perhaps, to make his presence known, — gave me a creepy sensation for a minute; and then, without saying a word to the fireman, I cut her back close to the centre, eased off my throttle, that she might not gain too rapidly in speed, and went out on the running-board. There was surely a body there lying crosswise and close up to the smoke-box door; I could see the legs stretched out motionless on my side; hanging on to the hand-rail, I stepped down on the steam-chest, and peered as far round as I could; there lay a fellow at full length, his head resting on his hand, riding along comfortably and smoking an old stub of a clay pipe.

"Hey!" said I; "hey!"

He turned his head leisurely in my direction, but made no answer nor did he appear to move. The train was now gathering headway, and I feared every moment that he would be pitched off and ground under the wheels; so I shouted to him to get up and come into the cab. He very leisurely straightened himself up and followed me back, much to the evident surprise of the fireman, who had anxiously peered out to see what had become of me.

I told him to sit on the box behind me, which he did without a word; having got the train adjusted to its gait, and having a long stretch of good running-ground ahead, I turned and asked him how he came on my front end.

"Got on when you was comin' slow up the hill."

"Where are you going?"

"West."

"West? Well, where is west? Some people call this west."

"Oh, I dunno; west is all I know; when I started I thought I'd go west somewheres an' grow up with the country, but I've 'bout concluded not to bother; the further I go, the more I git disgusted with everything. I see so many men that have had just about the same experience that I have, an' they all say they'll never be any man's slave ag'in, an' I believe they're 'bout right. What does the man have that works, anyway? In the first place he's got to humble himself an' worry his everlastin' soul-case out to git a job, an' then when he's got it, his trouble's only just begun: bosses never know when a man has done enough. The first thing it's a reduction of pay, or a lay off, or somebody offers to do it for less money; an' just as you've got yerself all settled down, to be a little comfortable, an' makin' plans for the future, you're on the outs ag'in; your dough-dish is upset, an' then there's more worry an' brain-fag, to hunt up another master; for that's just what it amounts to. An' what do you git for it? Stable room an' fodder—same's a car horse; that's all. Now I'm a tramp, no livin' man's my boss; nor I won't take a word o' clack from nobody neither—except policemen in the cities. I don't have to worry about where my grub is comin' from. If what I git at one house don't suit me, all I got to do is throw it away an' go to the next. I git plenty to eat, just as good as what other folks has; when I want clothes, all I've got to do is ask for 'em. I don't git the best, of course, but then I don't have to go much into society, and rags are always in fashion; an' you bet your sweet life I don't sleep outdoors, nor allow my health to be endangered by exposure to the elements. No, sir; I take good care of myself — better 'n I ever did in my life before. Why, young man, when I look back an' think of the thirty hard slavish years that I put in steamboatin' back there in the east, three hundred and sixty-five days to the year, night an' day, day an' night, well fed, to be sure, but never half sleep enough, scrimpin' an' savin', denyin' myself all the comforts, an' most of the necessaries of life, so 's to git ahead, an' then look at myself an' see what I've got to show for it, no wonder that I swear by the great god of thieves an' tramps that I'll never work ag'in."

"Surely," said I, "if as you say you worked and saved for thirty years, you must have accumulated something."

He looked steadily out of the window, and smoked furiously for some time; then knocking the ashes out of his pipe, he consigned it to some hidden receptacle in his ragged coat, and turning to me, said in a hard voice, and in language that was entirely devoid of slang, "Fifteen months ago, I wouldn't have sold out for five thousand dollars. I went steamboating when I was a boy, and, as I said, I worked and scrimped. Ten years ago I had a good job and a little money. I married the girl that I used to keep company with before I left home, and built a little house, just outside the city where I worked.

"I wasn't able to be at home much, but the thought of the wife and boy encouraged me to work, and I enjoyed my labor, knowing that it was for them.

"I worked for one man for fifteen years; he owned a large fleet of steam vessels of all kinds, from little bits of tugs to great big excursion boats. He is many times a millionnaire, has held high offices in the state, and is famed for his philanthropy. The money that he spends in charity in any one year would make you and me rich for life.

"I knew where there was an old steam lighter that could be bought cheap, and with a little fixing up be made serviceable; so when I saw a new factory in course of erection one day about ten miles out of town, I made inquiries, got acquainted with the owner, satisfied him that lighterage was cheaper than railroad transportation for his goods, and to make a long story short, made an agreement with him whereby I was to do his work by the month. He wouldn't make any longer agreement, because he said that if rates went down, he purposed to have the benefit of the lower prices.

"However, I was satisfied, for I knew I could do his work as cheaply as anybody; so I mortgaged my house, and with what money I had in bank I bought and fitted up the old lighter.

"When I resigned my job, my boss was very anxious to know the why and wherefore. I told him I thought I had a chance to better myself; and he said that although he hated to have his old employees leave him, still if I could better myself, he was glad of it, and if I needed any advice or help at any time, to let him know.

"I thanked him for his kindness, and started in business. I did first rate right from the start, made from thirty to fifty dollars a day clear, and was looking forward to the time when I should have my boat and home both clear of debt.

"I had only been running the job three weeks, when on my return to town one night I received a telegram, which read, 'Come home at once; Billy drowned.' That was my boy, the little eight-year-old fellow, that I thought more of than I did of my immortal soul. I put another captain in charge of my boat, and started for home with a heavy heart.

"Billy had been drowned while fishing for eels after dark. He was carried home, and when his mother saw her only child brought in dripping, his little hands hanging down, she swooned, and in falling, upset the tea table with the lamp upon it. Instantly the room was ablaze, and it was all the neighbors could do to drag the insensible form of my wife, fatally burned, out of the house.

"The house itself, with my child's remains, was totally consumed. A neighbor had sent me the news of Billy's death, thinking it best, I suppose, to deal the blow piecemeal. It was midnight when I got it, and two hours later when I stood half-crazed looking at the black spot on the ground where my home had been.

"They took me to my wife. She was delirious and unrecognizable. She died before daylight, and I buried her the same day. I went back to work, for my creditors must be paid. The next trip, when I returned to town, I met my former employer on the street. I thought that, having heard of my trouble, he was coming to express sympathy; for God knows I needed it badly enough.

"He walked up to me, a hard glitter in his eye, and said, —

"'I hear, Fielding, that you've gone into the transportation business.'

"'Yes, sir,' said I; 'in a small way.'

"'Small or big, you're in my way; do you understand? I won't tolerate any competition that I can crush, and I can crush you. Make the most of your contract, for when your month is up, you're done; and inside of three months I'll have your hide hanging on the fence.'

"When my month expired, my employer said he had made other arrangements, and would not need my boat. I asked permission to bid for the work. He took a paper from his desk, and said, 'Can you underbid that?' It was an offer from my former employer to carry his goods three months for nothing.

"The next month I didn't make money enough to pay expenses. The crew libelled the boat for their wages. My creditors swarmed round me like flies round a dead horse. When I could get nothing else, I could get plenty of what I never wanted before, — rum. I met my old boss one day when I was recovering from a long drunk, and asked him for a job. He told me he would have me arrested if I ever spoke to him in public again. That was the last straw. I snatched a rung from a near-by cart, and aimed a murderous blow at him; but in addition to his other accomplishments, he was a trained athlete. He wrenched it from me, nearly killed me with it, and then sent me to jail for three months for attempted atrocious assault and battery, while the newspapers printed editorials commenting on the dangerous state of society, when a gentleman could not run his own business to suit himself without taking the risk of a sandbagging from discharged employees.

"From the inmates of the workhouse I learned that my case was only one of hundreds. Men were surprised and laughed when they found that I thought my experience an unusual one. I had been so busy working all my life that I didn't know anything; but when I came out I had learned a new lesson, and now that I have time to observe what is going on in the world, I am convinced more and more every day that the workhouse philosophers were right: there *is* only a penny a day apiece for them that work and them that play; and they that play get both pennies. I tell you, my young friend, it's getting harder and harder for honest men to make a living in the east, and it will be the same here before long.

When one man gets control of a million dollars he can gobble up all the poor men and their earnings, that he has a mind to. They can't help themselves. And you mark my words, the time is not far off — you will probably live to see it — when the tramps will be thicker out here on these prairies than they are in the eastern cities now. I guess you're goin' slow enough, so 't I kin git off here. I don't care ter go in ter town ter night; folks might not be expectin' me. Gimme a chew o' terbaccer 'fore I go. Don't use it, hey? Good boy; you'll git over that all right. Wal, never mind. I kin find a cigar stub some'ers. So long."

I was slowed down to about ten miles per hour, entering the yard with its bewildering maze of signals and switches. He swung a moment on the step, and then dropped off. I glanced back, and saw him floundering over a frog; the corner of the head car hit him in the back, and he fell between it and the tender. I stopped as soon as possible. We extricated the dismembered remains and delivered them to the coroner. He was my first tramp, but how many times since have I had reason to remember his prophecy. In less than two years after that, the road was infested with them. The same grade where the ex-steamboat captain boarded me that night became a favorite resort for such as were bound westward, and it was a common occurrence for them to board the trains in sufficient numbers to enable them to defy the train hands.

Once a brakeman was thrown off the top of a car and killed by them. They frequently had revolvers, so that even if they were few, they were able to enforce their demands.

CHAPTER XIII

HELD UP — ON THE HEAD END OF A PASSENGER TRAIN — UNSATISFACTORY DIVIDENDS — A TEN PER CENT CUT — FRANK MANLY AND I ORGANIZE THE MEN

ONE night as I was running along at a good gait, crowding the speed limit a little, — for I was trying to make a certain siding ahead of the express, — some one shook me roughly by the shoulder, and said, "Hey, you!" I wondered that the fireman should be so energetic in addressing me; so it was in a fit of ill humor that I pulled my head in, and snarling out, "What do you want?" looked along the barrel of a big revolver, and into a pair of fierce eyes under the brim of a slouch hat. That was all I could see. But it was enough. I had scraped a hole in the paint on the gauge lamp globe, to read orders by, and the ray of light from it showed me this unpleasant sight. The cab being all in darkness, the gun and eyes appeared as if suspended in space.

There was also a voice, and it said, "I want you to slack up, right here, so's we kin git off."

"All right, sir," said I, and I shut right off. I reached for the whistle cord to call for brakes, but the voice said, "Hol' on, sonny; none o' that; 'tain't

"Looked along the barrel of a big revolver." — p. 200.

healthy;" so I let her roll. "Git outer the way till I see," said the voice, which, as the fireman had opened the door, I could now see belonged to a big, square-shouldered six-footer. He took my place at the window, and when she had slowed down sufficiently, I could hear voices in the rear counting one, two, three. They were counting themselves as they jumped off. The third man, after calling out his number, sang out, "All right." My friend with the ordnance climbed down on the step and dropped off without a word, and I went on. Presently the conductor came ahead to know why I had shut off. I told him to let off a gang of tramps. That night the express was half an hour late, and passed me in the siding, at the rate of seventy miles an hour.

She had been flagged near where my "tramps" got off. One fellow got on the engine, and entertained the engineer and fireman, while his three partners looted the express car, and took up a collection from the passengers.

After that, all freight engines and cabooses were furnished with arms, and as if by magic the tramps deserted our road for nearly a year, by which time the guns had become lost or stolen or useless, and gradually they returned, soon becoming as pestiferous as before. I don't think any of us would have used our arms though; for there are too many ways that they could have retaliated, and the ordinary risks of railroading are sufficient, without making deadly enemies of the countless horde of irresponsible vagabonds.

Owing to the efforts of a firm of real estate speculators, business began to boom on the road to such an extent that two new suburban trains were put on, calling for three passenger engineers, one for each engine, and one to swing between them, and take part of a day from each, as the miles and hours were too long.

I was one of the lucky three, and at last found myself in charge of the head end of a passenger train. The change was like coming out of the workhouse, to sit in a parlor for a living. The engines were kept clean, of course, the time was not fast, nor were the trains heavy, and every month I could tell beforehand just what my pay would be, unless some unforeseen accident occurred. Being the youngest, I had the relief. That didn't suit me very well, for an engineer always wants to *own* his engine, fix things to suit himself, and have no one to interfere with her. However, it was so very much better than any job I had ever had, that for some time I thought I had reached the very acme of my ambition, and would never ask for anything more; but I had not been on the train six months before a condition arose that was as unpleasant as it was unexpected. It seems that for a couple of years previously the road had not been paying satisfactory dividends, so the board of directors unseated the president and general manager, and filled those offices with others, pledged to retrenchment. The new policy made itself felt in our department at once.

The shop crews were reduced, and even those who were retained were put on short time. A howl went up at once; it was impossible to get work done on engines and cars, breakdowns on the road became the rule instead of, as heretofore, the exception; conductors and engineers had to do most of the repairing when in the sidetrack. The want of links and pins kept the train crews on the lookout for "iron." As brake-shoes were never renewed while a vestige remained, several wrecks were caused by inability to stop trains, any one of which cost the company more than all the brake-shoes used on the road in a year, and for once "no brakes" became, if not a valid, at least a reasonable excuse.

Cheap oil that would not lubricate cut out journals and crankpins, and besides the time lost on the road the cars and engines had to be laid up for want of shop men to repair them. Waste was no longer issued, so that the engines became coated with grease and dirt, making it next to impossible to detect a fracture in any of the parts. Under this reform administration, the quality of the fuel became so depreciated that it was impossible to make time, the first result of which was that engineers and firemen were suspended, and the next, that business fell off, for people would neither ship their goods nor travel on a road where the service was so unreliable.

Within three months two engines were wrecked, and their engineers killed by broken parallel rods tearing up through the cabs, like huge iron flails, and flogging them to death. In the suit for damages, brought by their widows, as it was proven that the men had reported the necessity of having the brasses in those rods reduced for weeks, but there were no men to do it, the company had to pay heavy damages. A broken driving-wheel tire ditched a passenger train — more damages.

Discontent was rampant; grumbling and cursing at the management became the order of the day. There was not a mile of safe track on the whole line. The wrecking train was hardly ever idle, and on more than one occasion it became necessary to send another train out to bring her in.

While we were laboring under these aggravating inconveniences, an order was posted on the bulletin board to the effect that after the first of the next month, all employees receiving one dollar and a half per day, or over, would be cut ten per cent until further notice.

This included engineers, firemen, conductors, and brakemen. The men gathered in knots and discussed the cut. The new management was cordially damned, and the question raised, "What shall we do about it?" As there appeared to be no prospect of the men arriving at an understanding by such disunited methods, Frank Manly, who had remained my firm friend and particular chum ever since the fight we had with Hussey about promotion, called for me one evening, and, during a long walk, we discussed the troubles existing on the road, and cud-

"The wrecking train was hardly ever idle."—p.

gelled our brains for a remedy, with the result that we agreed that nothing could be done until all employees who were affected by the cut could be got together to argue the question, adopt resolutions, and send a representative committee to the front with them.

Near the round-house there was a hotel, which depended almost entirely on the patronage of the railroaders, the upper floor of which was a large hall, used for balls, concerts, and so forth. We decided that we should be perfectly safe in calling a meeting there without consulting Schroeder (the proprietor). As it was not desirable that we should appear as ringleaders in the matter, we adjourned to my room, and drew up two notices, as follows:—

NOTICE.

All employees of this road, engaged in train service, who are dissatisfied with bulletin order No. 3, of June 14th, which orders a reduction of ten per cent in all salaries of $1.50, or over, are requested to meet at Schroeder's assembly room on the evening of July 1st, at 8.15, sharp. By order of

THE COMMITTEE.

These we printed with pen and ink, so as to make it impossible for any one to trace our handwriting; for, never having written anything of importance before, we had an exaggerated idea of our present undertaking.

We dated the meeting three days ahead, to give the men who were at the other end of the division a chance to see the notice on their return, and so get all hands to talking about it. Frank was to go out at twelve o'clock that night, so it was agreed that he should make it his business to post one copy on the round-house bulletin board, while I would hand the other to a conductor whom we felt that we could trust and get him to do the same on their board.

The next day excitement ran high. Who were "the committee"? Who had appointed them? "Are ye goin' to the meetin'?" We began to feel a little alarmed at the evident magnitude of the movement we had started, but we met in a secluded place at the other end of the division next day, and bolstered each other's courage by declaring that we were delighted with the prospects of an enthusiastic meeting, and promised each other to see the thing through now that it had started so auspiciously. I saw Schroeder that night and promised to take up a collection to pay for the room and light, guaranteeing to make good myself any shortage that might result.

When the time arrived, Frank and I strolled down to the hotel. Jake had faithfully performed his part, the room was brilliantly illuminated and filled with chairs, but with the exception of ourselves, not a railroader was in sight, although it was always a favorite lounging-place, and for some time past had been especially well patronized by the disgruntled. Half-past eight — nine o'clock — half-past nine — this would never do; we each started in a different direction to see if we could round up enough men to make a showing, agreeing to return in half an hour.

I went directly to the conductors' "hangout," a large waiting-room off the despatcher's office. I found fifteen or twenty men — conductors and brakemen — discussing the proposed meeting. I entered into the conversation and soon found that not a man of them dared take part in it, or even express himself in favor of it, for fear that he would lose his job. I soon assumed a leading part in the conversation, and they grouped themselves around me, while I gave them an exhortation that would have done credit to a camp meeting. I told them that we were being robbed of our hard earnings, in order that our wages might be used to pay dividends to wealthy stockholders, who had never strained a muscle or shed a drop of sweat to make the road a success, while we had been doing that very thing for years. I told them that if the road was not a financial success, it was no fault of ours, and we were not obliged to pay for the blunders of the management. When the road was paying big dividends they never thought of sharing them with us by raising our pay, but any excuse was good enough for a reduction.

I told them that while the amount taken from us would impoverish us greatly, it would not add to the already luxurious living of the stockholders a single case of champagne, or a new suit of livery for their flunkies. I reminded them that this same unpractical new management had, by their penny-wise, and pound-foolish operation of the road, lost patronage, and incurred costly damage suits, which they now called upon us — who on account of that same silly management were working harder than ever before — to pay for out of our wages, and to the knee-quaking argument that any man who took part in the movement would be blacklisted, discharged, and damned forevermore, I told them, that if only half a dozen had the manhood to stand out and protest against the outrage, I had no doubt that hell would be their portion. "But," said I, "if we all turn out and make a unanimous demonstration, our very numbers will protect us, for they can't discharge a whole division. Certainly no man has so far made himself so conspicuous in this movement as I have right here to-night, and I am not afraid to go to that meeting, or to act on a committee, and tell the president just what I have told you. Now then" — looking at my watch — "the engineers and firemen are waiting for you at the hall; they are determined not to submit to this reduction without a protest; I have been sent here to ask you to coöperate with us in righting this great wrong. Remember that in the meeting you will have all the chance in the world to express your opinions, and to win as many to your way of thinking as you can, and if you are dissatisfied with the action taken, you can withdraw and refuse to give it your sanction. I ask that every man here who desires to have his wages reduced, or who thinks he ought to be made to contribute to a fund to make good the losses due to bungling management, to hold up his hand."

A careful inspection failed to reveal a single hand raised. "That's enough," said I; "come on, we're late now." And at the head of my partly enthusiastic and partly weak-kneed recruits I started for the hall. During my impromptu remarks, the crowd had more than trebled, men dropping in every minute from the cabooses and hotels, so that as far as numbers were concerned, I had a crowd of sixty or seventy men; but I knew them, and was not over-elated at my success, for the genuine railroader, although he would like exceedingly to possess the earth and the fulness thereof, is so everlastingly afraid of losing his job, that he submits to impositions that would cause a revolt in a Chinese laundry, contenting himself with damning the company in a low voice from behind the coal-pile, or in the seclusion of his home, while a nod of recognition from the division superintendent, or the mention of his first name by the master mechanic, sets his heart to fluttering with ardent self-congratulations.

On the way to the hall, several old gray-headed, chin-whiskered fellows, veteran employees, surrounded me, and asked me what *I* was "goin' to dew?" They advised me to be "mighty careful," or the first thing I knew I would be out of a job; they guessed that I would find before I was through with it, that the road belonged to the company, and that they would run it to suit themselves, for all of me and my crowd.

"All right," said I; "I have no objection to their

running the road to suit themselves, but I'll be hanged if I'm a slave, and when it comes to a question affecting my wages, I propose to be heard."

This sentiment met with vociferous approval from the younger and radical element, but the conservatives shook their heads, and wisely predicted that I should find out that I couldn't dictate to a railroad company.

As we approached the hall I was filled with anxiety, wondering how Frank had succeeded with the engineers and firemen. There were fifteen or twenty of them standing in a group outside the door, talking in a half-frightened way, as if they considered the idea of asserting that they had any rights in the matter, to be equivalent to high treason.

My arrival with such a strong body of reinforcements seemed, however, to hearten them, and when I spoke up with an assumption of fearless cheerfulness, saying, "Step right inside, gentlemen, the meeting is about to commence," they obeyed with alacrity.

I stepped to the chair, rapped on the table with my knuckles, asking them to please come to order, and remove their hats. I then stated briefly why the meeting had been called, told them there was no necessity for any man committing himself any farther than he saw fit to do; but added that, personally, I was in favor of resisting the reduction with all the power at our command; for, I warned them, if we submitted to this initial stab at our inalienable rights as American citizens to have a voice in the adjustment of our rate of pay, we might expect it to be quickly followed by further encroachments. I warmed with my subject, reminding them that in defence of a similar cause, our forefathers had shed their blood and laid down their lives at Lexington and Bunker Hill.

When the applause following this patriotic outburst had subsided, I moved the election of Mr. Frank Manly as permanent chairman. The motion was seconded by a dozen at once, and, seeing Frank getting on his feet to decline, I put the question, and he was unanimously elected *vivâ voce*. I called on the oldest engineer and conductor present by name to escort Mr. Manly to the chair, and was pleased to observe the alacrity with which they obeyed. They were already beginning to feel that wholesome *esprit de corps*, without which no movement can succeed.

As I resigned the chair to Frank, he said in an undertone, "What in thunder did you do that for? I don't know how to preside at a meeting."

"Sh! be still," said I. "You know as much about it as any of us. Accept all motions that are made, let them debate as long as they have a mind to, and, when nobody has any more to say, put it to a vote and announce it lost or carried, whichever way you think it ought to go." Frank grinned dubiously, and I left him, taking a seat in the audience.

I had no sooner taken my seat than a great buzzing ensued,—every man talking eagerly to his neighbor; so, seeing there was no prospect of accomplishing anything unless somebody made a motion, I rose and moved that we proceed to organize by electing officers. As the meeting readily assented to this, but made no attempt to do it, I found it necessary to nominate a secretary and sergeant-at-arms, explaining what their duties were. We soon became organized; the sergeant-at-arms was directed to keep the door closed, but to admit all employees of the road and no others. It was encouraging to observe that the door was kept pretty constantly on the swing, admitting men; it was evident that the news had got abroad and was already exciting interest. In order to get the business started, I now moved that a committee be elected,—consisting of one engineer, one fireman, one conductor, a brakeman, and switchman,—to call on the general manager and protest against the reduction. This had the desired effect,—it started debate; but the great trouble now was to keep them in order. They all wanted to talk at once; and seeing that Frank was perplexed by his unfamiliar duties, I went to him and told him to explain that they must address the chair, and only the person recognized could speak, and that he must not be interrupted until through. Frank begged me to take the chair, saying that he didn't understand it and didn't want it; but I told him that he was the duly elected chairman and was doing all right. While we were discussing this point, an old freight conductor arose in the rear of the hall and roared out: "Mr. Chairman! what's that man doin' up there with you? Seems ter me he's takin' a good deal on himself. I guess we're all jest as much interested as he is, ain't we? I don't want no one-man business here; let him come down out o' that!" Although the remarks were not flattering, I was glad to hear them, for it showed that an interest was being taken in the proceedings.

We made but little real progress that night beyond organizing and exciting debate. The motion to elect a committee did not reach a vote. Shortly before adjourning, a slight ripple of excitement was caused by the round-house foreman and yard-master seeking admission. The sergeant-at-arms, big with the importance of his new office, slammed the door in their faces, admonishing them to get out. Frank asked what the trouble was, and Mike replied: "A couple o' spies, your honor, tryin' ter git in here an' find out what's goin' on." While he was making his report to the chair, the "spies" were pounding on the door. I made a motion that, as they were employees and subject to the cut as well as ourselves, they be admitted and requested to join us.

A hot debate ensued for a few minutes. We didn't want any petty officers spying on us and reporting our acts to the bosses, they said; but I reminded them that as we intended to report our acts to the general manager ourselves, they could not possibly do us any harm, and besides if we refused to admit them, they would go away in anger and report that we were evidently doing something that we were afraid to have known. It was finally agreed that a committee of three should interview them and decide.

I was appointed on the committee.

We found the two gentlemen in the anteroom in rather bad humor; we told them the object of the meeting, and asked if they were in sympathy with the movement. They said that they didn't relish a reduction of pay any more than ourselves, but wanted to know how we were going to help it? We told them that that was a matter for the men to decide for themselves, and that we had not got as far as that yet. They finally accepted our invitation to come in and take part in the meeting, under the assurance that they would be allowed to withdraw if the action of the majority failed to meet with their approval. Shortly after this the meeting adjourned until the next evening.

The next day excitement ran high on the road. The news quickly spread to the other divisions, that the men on the Chicago division were organizing to resist the reduction. On our division the passenger crews, both of engines and trains, who had taken but little part in the meeting, began to ask questions, and offer advice. The passenger man, conductor or engineer, having passed through the severe preliminary training of the freight service, and reached the summit of his calling, is always a conservative. He has arrived at the railroad man's "easy street," and he knows that if he loses that passenger train, it will be years, if ever, before he will get another. He doesn't want to lose the best job he ever had, knowing that besides the uncertainty of getting another job of any kind, there is the positive fact that he will not get another passenger train without working his way drearily through the freight business, and one experience on freight is enough to satisfy the cravings of any man, even though he were a human hog.

They are not so very much to be blamed, these passenger men; for human nature is weak, and we have no right to demand that every man shall be a self-sacrificing martyr. Even with a twenty-five per cent reduction, they would make a better and easier living than they could pounding an old freight train on some other road.

I was up the road when the next meeting occurred, and Frank was only able to stay long enough to initiate his successor into the mysteries of controlling the turbulent elements of which the meeting was composed.

The entire evening was used up in futile arguments, recriminations, and personalities, and finished up with a fight among a half-dozen brakemen. Several chairs were broken, and the landlord refused to allow us to enter the hall again until he was paid for his furniture. A hasty collection satisfied his claim, and once more we renewed our deliberations. Frank made an excellent opening speech, in which he deplored the lost time, and assured them that he would keep order if he had to personally eject every man from the hall. His speech had the desired effect, and we got to work at once. I started in to nominate members for the committee, and was both surprised and disgusted at the unanimity with which the honor was declined. Axiom: The average railroad man would rather not serve on a committee for fear he will lose his job.

At last an old fellow jumped up after I had nominated half a dozen unwilling candidates, and bawled out, "Sa-ay! you've nominated about everybody in the room to serve on this committee, an' now by gum I nominate you." There was a roar of laughter at this, and as soon as it subsided, I turned to the chairman, and said, "I accept." This brought down the house; when the cheering was over I nominated the previous speaker, and amid more noise he accepted. After this we had but little trouble in completing our committee. As chairman I demanded the most explicit instructions, declining on behalf of myself and fellow-committeemen to assume the responsibility of formulating the demands to be made on the company.

While this subject was under debate the sergeant-at-arms in answer to an alarm at the outer door, reported to the chairman, that two committees from the other two divisions of the road sought admission. They were admitted amid great enthusiasm, and

"'Sa-ay! you've nominated about everybody.'"—p. 216.

stated that they wished to take part with us in any proceedings which we might take, looking to the righting of the wrong that had been done to all hands.

At first it seemed that we should have to reconstruct our grievance committee in order that it should contain representatives of the entire road; but as they assured us that the men whom they represented were willing to go to any length to defeat the obnoxious arts of the new management, it was finally agreed that they should have a voice, and a vote equal to two-thirds of the whole on the instruction of the committee, and in return, they would delegate our committee to represent their interests. As it was getting late, and the matter had been pretty thoroughly discussed, the meeting was adjourned for twenty-four hours, to enable the crews now on the road to have their say.

The next evening the full instructions were adopted, and were as follows: The committee were to call on the president or his representative at the earliest opportunity, and request that the rates of pay existing previous to the issuing of the ten per cent order be restored. They were to make no threats; to use only such arguments as they could think of; and to accept no compromise. Having carried out these instructions, they were to report back to the meeting.

CHAPTER XIV

IN THE PRESIDENT'S OFFICE — CURSING OUR ENTHUSIASTIC FOLLY — THE DREAD OF DISCHARGE — A FOXY OLD DUCK — RETALIATIONS — OFFICERS PAID IN FULL — WE STRIKE

THE next day at eleven o'clock, we sat dressed in our best clothes in the anteroom of the president's office, waiting for an answer to our request for an audience. I have not the slightest doubt that every man on that committee fully believed that he had worked his last day on the road; I know I did.

Presently the door of the spacious private office was thrown wide open, and we were requested to enter. Hats in hands, and hearts in mouths, we filed in, I, by virtue of my office as chairman, at the head. Standing in the middle of the room, both hands in his pockets, his feet spread wide apart, and with an extremely fragrant cigar cocked at an angle of forty-five towards his left eye, was a tall, gray, spare man, plainly but expensively dressed, who regarded us rather superciliously as we awkwardly drew up before him. This was the president, the highest railroad functionary that any of us had ever seen. We firmly believed his power to be greater than that of any Czar. When we at last got ourselves shuffled into some kind of order before him, he ran his eye keenly along our rank, and said, —

"Well, gentlemen, I understand that you are a committee, representing the employees of my road. Which is your chairman?"

I told him that I was the chairman.

"Ah, yes! what is your name, please?"

I told him.

"And your occupation?"

"Engineer."

"Yes? very well; now you may introduce your committee, please, giving their names and occupations."

As I called out their names, I could see each individual committeeman shrink and shrivel under the keen critical glance of the magnate, who evidently regarded us as imbeciles or freaks, an odd lot to be studied a bit, wheedled into subjection if possible, but under no circumstances to be allowed to interfere with his financial policy.

And the committee! I know that every mother's son of them was cursing the enthusiastic folly that caused him to accept the appointment.

There was no applauding constituency here to keep their spirits up; only that grim old financier in the foreground, who could discharge us all as easily as he could take the next puff of his cigar.

And here I may as well explain to the general reader why it is that railroad men have such a great dread of discharge, for it is a fact that they fear it more than they do death. The average railroader has started at the business as a boy, consequently he has never known anything but railroading. The first lesson he learned was, that the general manager, if not the president, started in just where he is now. The next, that every day that he remains in the company's employ he is one day nearer to a better job; for promotion is the rule on all railroads. The next, that if he is discharged, he becomes almost absolutely ineligible for employment in the railroad business; as, when seeking employment, he must furnish his pedigree; and even if he is employed to fill an urgent vacancy, the telegraph immediately asks the superintendent of the road from whence he came, *not* "why was this man discharged?" but "have you any objection to our employing him?" If the answer is in the affirmative, the instant that his services can be dispensed with he is notified of that fact; also, should he be allowed to remain in the new situation, it is bound to be a lower grade in the service than that from which he was discharged, and as promotion is exceedingly slow, owing to the very fact that the men hang so tenaciously to their positions, — never under any circumstances resigning, he has to look forward to the cheerful prospect of years of hard service before he can regain a position equivalent to that from which he was discharged, probably for no fault of his own.

Then, again, from the very nature of their employment, they are usually compelled to live isolated from the general community; near the round-houses, shops, and yards where they are employed. Being steady, hard-working men, with tolerably regular incomes, and the hope of permanent employment and promotion, they are induced to mortgage their salaries for years in advance to build homes for themselves and families; and, on account of their hazardous calling, they usually carry all the life and accident insurance that they are able to, at enormously heavy rates. Consequently, discharge, which usually upsets all these plans for the future welfare of those dependent on him, generally finds the railroad man with only such ready money as is left from his last month's pay, after deducting the amounts due on his home and policy, and with the prospect before him of having to go hundreds and even thousands of miles to get another job. The home, on which he has been paying every cent that he could spare for years, must be sacrificed to the sharks, who are always on the lookout for just such bargains; while he, fortunate if after months of search he obtains employment in an inferior position, and at reduced pay, has to work, and save, and scrimp for months, in order to forward enough money to the family to keep them alive, and at the same time provide a new home for them, together with transportation for them and their household goods.

Reduced again to poverty, with a family on his hands, is it any wonder that he dreads discharge more than he does death? That, at least, is oblivion.

The brief ceremony of introduction over, he asked,

with a cynical smile, "Well, gentlemen, what can I do for you?" I told him our errand, and he asked if we thought we were more competent to manage the property than he was. Remembering that he was the president, I lyingly told him no. I told him that we didn't expect or wish to manage the property, but that we were working harder than we had ever done before, and getting less pay, which we didn't consider just.

He said that circumstances, which we would not be able to understand, had reduced the earning capacity of the road so that it was unable to pay the interest on its bonds, and pay the wages we had heretofore received. He said that if the investors didn't get satisfactory returns for their money they would have the road put in the hands of a receiver; and then we should be paid in scrip, which we should have to sell for what anybody chose to give for it. Did we think we should be any better off then?

I said, "We don't think—" "Hold on, young man," said he, "you're doing altogether too much of the talking. I want to hear from some of the others. Then pointing to the old conductor, who had nominated me on the committee, he said, "You're an old railroad man, and, I presume, a man of family; which would you prefer to do, take home your pay at the end of the month in cash, and, by sacrificing ten per cent for a short time, help to put the road on a paying basis, or receive your pay in scrip, which you would have to sell for perhaps twenty-five per cent, or more, less than its face value, for an indefinite time?"

"I can't pay my bills with what I'm gittin' now," said the old fellow.

The president bit his lip, and flushed at the miscarriage of his attempt to flatter the old man into becoming his ally, and said with ill-suppressed anger, "I'm afraid the exhorbitant wages that you men have been receiving heretofore have induced you to live extravagantly; you should economize; I have to. My salary has been reduced in the same proportion as yours, but I don't go to the board of directors and complain; I accept the situation, and am willing to accept even a further reduction, if necessary, to enable the road to pull through. You men don't understand the situation."

"Probably," said Denny King, the fireman, "you get more now than all of us put together."

"Yes, I presume I do. Presidents are usually paid a higher salary than firemen. But come, I haven't time to stand here talking all day. What do you men want? What is it that you expect me to do?"

"We were sent here, sir, by all the men engaged in train service, to ask you to restore our pay, and they will expect an answer from you. What are we to tell them?" said I.

"You will tell them that I cannot possibly do so, at this time. But as soon as the earnings of the road will warrant the extra expense, I will consider the matter."

"Then you won't promise that we shall ever get it?" said I.

He was angry again, we could see that; but he controlled himself, thought a moment, and then said: "You may tell them from me that every man, from the president down, has been included in this reduction of salaries; that I *hope* it will be only a temporary necessity, and that when the time comes to restore them, the restoration shall begin with the lowest-salaried employees, and I will be the last to benefit by it. I can say no more now. If that isn't satisfactory to you, you'll have to do whatever you see fit.

Turning his back to us, he sat down and began to write. Seeing that there was no more to be said, we walked out without so much as saying good-day. When we got out on the street, all hands commenced to volubly denounce the president.

"Say, did you ever see such a foxy old duck? A lot we made by goin' to him. He's willing to submit to another reduction, if necessary. Of course. Why not? It's only takin' the money out of one pocket to put it in the other, with him. He'll 'consider it.' That ain't a very rash promise! Blast him! Who is he, anyway, I wonder?"

"Oh, some eastern bank president that's got the deadwood on the road."

"No, he ain't. I know all about him. He was a conductor on a Boston horse car. He married the president's daughter, and his father-in-law made him superintendent. Then it wasn't but a short time till he owned the road, bankrupted the old man, and got a divorce from his wife. Now he's probably bought stock enough in this road to get himself elected president, and he's playing a game of freeze-out. Nothing would suit him better than to have a strike. It would help him to knock the stock down, and then he'd buy it in cheap. That's what he's up to."

"Well, d—n him, anyway. May lightnin' strike him, is the best wish I have for him."

We made our report to the meeting that evening, and a furious debate followed. Some were for striking at once; others thought we should give the president every chance to show his hand before resorting to extreme measures. They argued that he had not positively refused to restore our pay; that we had no right to brand him as a liar without proof; that there might be a great deal more in what he said about the road not paying expenses than we were aware of, and that at any rate he was entitled to be believed until proven unworthy. Nobody, they said, would justify us in striking on such grounds as we now had; and, at any rate, we could always do that, if it came to the worst. There was no necessity to be in such a terrible hurry to throw up our jobs. The times were hard, and half a loaf was better than no bread; besides, if some of the members of the committee were right, a strike was just what he wanted, and we should be fools to play into his hand.

A vote was taken on the sense of the meeting, and it was shown that nearly three-fourths of those present were in favor of giving the company ample time to show whether they intended to deal fairly by us or not. It was also recommended that we make our organization permanent, and hold monthly meetings hereafter. These two resolutions had to be submitted to the other side at their meeting the following evening; and as they indorsed them, the trains continued to roll without interruption.

This flurry having passed successfully, the timid, or, if you choose, "conservative," element now began to join the organization with the avowed purpose of controlling it, and preventing any more such dangerous propaganda as that from which we had so narrowly escaped.

But it would seem that the president was indeed bent on having trouble; for now there commenced a series of discharges for the most trivial causes, and the victims were not the radicals, either, but they were almost invariably the conservative old fellows who had been for years in the employ of the company, who had the best trains, and considered themselves fixtures. They were the kind who wisely told us that we mustn't think that we could dictate to a railroad company; and as they seemed to consider themselves particularly charged with maintaining the company's dignity, but little sympathy was felt for them, as one after another their heads were lopped off, and we, the radicals, succeeded to their jobs.

The oldest engineer on the road set up his wedges. One of them stuck on the trip out that night, the box got hot, he lost ten minutes with it, and was fired when he returned. The allowance of oil was reduced, until it was almost impossible to get over the division. At the same time, strict orders were issued that no stores must be drawn at the other end. A passenger engine got a hot engine truck-box. The engineer had no waste to pack it with. He used all the oil he had on it, lost time at every water-plug cooling it, and finally, just as he rolled into the depot, the wheel dropped off. He was discharged. An old conductor, a deacon in the church of which the president was a shining light, turned in twelve cents *too much* at the end of his run, and was rewarded with a blue envelope, entitling him — a man of sixty — to look for a job braking on freight, throwing switches in some yard, or flagging a road crossing, at thirty dollars per month, *if* he could get it.

Soon the "conservatives" could be counted on the fingers of an armless man. They outradicalled the radicals. As their ardor increased, ours cooled. We asked them how they liked it; we reminded them that not so very long ago they were stanch supporters of the company, when we needed their assistance; but now we were doing very well, thank you, the good jobs were coming our way, and we were making more money than we did previous to the cut, and getting jobs that we had never expected to be able to touch with a forty-foot pole. They asked us if we thought it was right to take the trains they had hauled for so many years. "Certainly! why not? You are all getting discharged, and somebody's got to have them, and they come to us by right of seniority, the same as they did to you." We told them these things merely to aggravate them, but not being fossils we knew very well that the company was simply using us to club each other with, and that our turn would come just as surely as theirs had.

Matters had been going on like this for nearly a year, when a rumor began to circulate that the general officers had been put on full pay again. If this was true, it was a most flagrant case of deliberate lying on the president's part, that could be conceived; of course we had no means of proving it, but inside of two months the whole story was given in one of the daily papers in a signed article. We called a special meeting to consider this new grievance. By this time there was no division of opinion. The committee were unanimously instructed to give the president three hours to restore the wages of every man on the road, and if he failed, a word that had been agreed upon was to be sent by telegraph to every conductor and engineer on the road, or at work in the yards. A switchman was named in each yard to receive the word, and he was to post it on the bulletin board in the yard-master's office, besides giving it verbally to all the men whom he could reach. The receipt of the word "Rain" constituted a notice for every man to stop work at 4 P.M. on the following day, no matter where he should be. All engines were to cut loose from their trains, draw their fires, run as far from the train as possible, blow out the boiler, and empty the tank, filling the firebox to the crown-sheet with green coal. The crews were then to leave them, and make their way home as best they could. Conductors and brakemen of passenger trains were to stay with their trains, and care for their passengers as long as any remained on board, or until relieved. Switchmen were to securely spike all switches in their charge and go home. No striking employee would be allowed to trespass on the company's property during the continuance of the strike.

It was acknowledged on the part of the men that if we once struck, many of us must expect to lose our positions; but matters had become so unbearable on the road lately, that few cared what the result would be. A petty tyrannical system of fines and suspensions had been inaugurated, which, together with our reduced rate of pay, kept us in such poverty that we began to fear actual starvation; everybody had got as deeply in debt as he could, and the keepers of stores, boarding-houses, and saloons, who were nearly as badly off as ourselves, sympathized with us, and promised to help all they could.

The same committee was again sent to interview

the president. This time we were not admitted to the inner office; he stepped out into the anteroom, and asked us our business. I reminded him of his promise: that when wages were restored, he would begin at the lowest-salaried man, and remain until the last himself. "Well, what of it?" said he. I handed him the paper, and asked if the article to which I pointed was true. He glanced over it rapidly, his face flushed to the roots of his hair; and slapping the paper viciously with the back of his left hand, he said, with his teeth clenched and the words hissing through them like steam through a leaky stuffing-box, "This is the most outrageous insult to which I was ever subjected. What do you mean by coming here with this filthy rag? Do you realize that you are accusing me of wilful, deliberate lying?"

I told him that we had made no accusation; but, seeing the statement with the author's name attached, we had concluded that there must be something in it, or if not, that he would thank us for having called his attention to it so that he might punish the slanderer; and anyhow, we had been sent to him to ask for a restoration of our pay.

He glared at me like a wild beast; I thought he would jump at my throat, but controlling himself with an effort, he said, "I told you men when you were here before, that when the financial condition of the road warranted the restoration of the former rate of pay, I would consider the matter. When that time comes, and I have considered it, you will be informed of my decision."

The brakeman on the committee chipped in here, and asked him if the report in the paper, that the general officers, including himself, had had their pay restored, was true or not?

"I don't think you know to whom you are talking. I will not be catechised. When I have any communication to make to the employees, it will be made in the usual manner, by means of an order."

He was about to return to his sanctum, and seeing that there was absolutely no hope of getting anything out of him I said, "One moment, sir, if you please; we are not through yet. Our orders are to notify you that unless an order restoring our pay appears within three hours, we will resign in a body."

"Who are *we?*"

"Every employee in the train service of this railroad."

"Very well. I can't help it; and as for this committee, you can consider yourselves discharged now, and I shall issue orders at once to have any of you who may be found trespassing on the company's property arrested, and lodged in prison."

"The h—ll you will, you bean-eatin', psalm-singin', son of a down-east Jew," said old Merrill, the conductor. The door slammed, and he was gone; at the same time a policeman appeared from somewhere, and ordered us out of the building. We went, making a great deal of unnecessary noise, for we were mad clear through, and being discharged, neither owed nor showed allegiance or respect to our late president or the property under his control.

For the next half or three-quarters of an hour we kept a telegraph operator busy sending the word "Rain" to innumerable addresses all along the line. There was no occasion to report. All hands would know the result of our interview before sundown, and as we were certainly out of it, we had no more interest in the fight now than any other spectators.

The next day at four o'clock in the afternoon every wheel stopped, and every locomotive fire was dumped on more than seven hundred miles of railroad, including branches and leased lines. The men were a unit, and the paralysis was perfect.

That night the road was dead. The next morning the papers blazed with accounts of the strike and advertisements for help. Engineers, firemen, railroad men of any kind, laborers who never saw a railroad, anybody that could work, could find permanent employment and good wages at the office of the superintendent of the —— railroad.

The clerks in the offices were hustled out into the yard, and made to sweat and lacerate their delicate hands, tear and soil their cloths, and injure their tender feelings, by pulling spikes from switches, clawing the green coal out of the fireboxes, dragging heavy and "narsty" hoses to the engines, and forming bucket and cordwood brigades, while we sat on the fences and cheered them on to their unaccus-

"The clerks in the offices were hustled out into the yard." — p. 232.

tomed and unwelcomed toil by such remarks as never fail to present themselves to the mind under such circumstances. The new employees, as fast as hired, were sent to help. Their appearance and awkward manner of going about the work offered fresh subjects for our witticisms. Their patience must have been sorely tried. From jeering it was but a short step to throwing various missiles. The clerks dodged in fear and trembling, but the laborers talked back, and gave threat for threat, sarcasm for sarcasm.

At length a half a brick struck a burly Irishman in the small of the back as he was straining at the clawbar to draw a spike. He straightened up a moment, rubbed his sore back, and then with a yell of rage, he started for a grinning crowd with the heavy clawbar. It was the one spark necessary to kindle a furious conflagration. I have said that the whole population of the locality sympathized with us. They were out in force, and when the interloper resented what was considered to be his just deserts, he found that he had stirred up a hornet's nest. The crowd having once broken loose, charged through the yard, driving everything before them. Before the police arrived a dozen fires were started in as many different places; and owing to the impossibility of getting the fire engines through the yard, over fifteen hundred cars, many of them loaded with valuable merchandise, were burned to the ground before the flames could be extinguished, and seven locomotives, their tanks and boilers empty, were completely ruined. The night shut down on a dreary scene of smoking desolation, where but the day before the air had rung with the cheerful sounds of busy commerce. The sheriff telegraphed to the governor for troops, saying that he was unable to control the mob. The next morning militiamen were patrolling the yard, and the work proceeded with no further interruptions than an occasional jeering by the onlookers at the awkward attempts of the new men, to get the few remaining dead engines watered and fired-up.

In the meantime there was the very old Harry to pay up the road. At W——, where I once had such a time weighing coal cars, three locomotives had been run into the turn-table pit. A rock cut, about a mile west of the station, had been choked by tumbling its natural walls into itself. This was accomplished by dropping cartridges into the seams and cracks along the top on both sides, and exploding them; the natural consequence being that huge blocks were split off, and tumbled into the cut. The idea was to close the road, and prevent the passage of trains, but after the job was done, it occurred to the perpetrators that there was a branch that would enable them to run around the obstruction; so a hand-car was loaded with rendrock, and four men took it to an iron bridge five miles farther east, and before the second morning of the strike dawned, the bridge lay in the creek, and the road was most effectually "cut in two."

I heartily disapproved of this violence and destruction; not from any quixotic sentiment on the company's account, but because I knew it could do nothing but harm to the interests of the men. Although I was discharged, and could never expect to work on the road again, there were many elderly married men that I hoped would be reinstated after the trouble was over; but if the rioters continued to destroy property, it was sure to be blamed on the employees, whether rightly or not, and would make it next to impossible for any of them to be taken back.

I went among them and advised them to remember the order issued by the organization, that all employees should refrain from trespassing on the company's property. I was assured by all the men I saw that they had obeyed the order strictly, and I believe that as a rule they had, but I will not go to the extent of claiming that none of them took any part in the rioting, for railroad men are far from angelic, and many of them had cause to hate every rail and spike in the road.

CHAPTER XV

THE PRESIDENT SWEARS OUT WARRANTS — WE GO EAST — STRAPPED IN BUFFALO — DRUNK AND DISORDERLY — WE HOOF IT — LEVYING ON THE FARMERS — A MOVABLE FEAST

IT took them three days to get the trains in. Then, with such men as they could pick up, they began to operate the road — after a fashion. The president, having now presumably recovered from the first shock of the strike, swore out warrants for the arrest of all the members of the committee. Not caring to gratify the gentleman's animosity by serving the state at his request, I left town between two days, in company with my chum, Frank Manly. We both had a few hundred dollars; and as we knew that the vicinity of Chicago would be anything but a sanitarium for us for a long time to come, we decided to go east, and see what manner of country it was that had produced our president.

We had both been working steadily for years, so that our enforced holiday was not entirely unwelcome, and when we got as far as Buffalo, feeling that we were now safe from our enemy, we determined to celebrate a bit, as young fellows sometimes will. Either we were unfortunate in our choice of entertainment, or else we bore the indelible mark of strangers about us; for the result of our first night's amusement was that we were robbed of every cent, and in the fight that ensued between us and the robbers, *we* were arrested while they escaped. As we had been pretty roughly handled, our faces cut and bruised, and our clothing torn to rags, we made a pretty tough looking pair, when we were brought before the police magistrate next morning.

"What's the charge, officer?"

"Drunk and disorderly; they were creating a disturbance in Canal Street, fighting, your honor."

"Which way?" (To us.)

"Sir?" said Frank.

"Which way are you two tramps going? east, or west."

"We're not tramps, sir, we're —"

"Which way are you going? Come, out with it."

"We were on our way east, sir, to —"

"Well, continue on your way east. I'll give you thirty minutes to get out of town, and if you come before me again, I'll give you thirty days in the workhouse. Next!"

The policeman gave us a shove out of the door with a "G'wan now — clear out!"

Doggedly and shamefaced, we sauntered along, beginning to feel already the character that we looked. Presently Frank burst into a hearty laugh. I asked him what in thunder he found so awfully amusing? "Why," said he, "we came east to see the country; didn't we? What better chance could we have to see it, than by tramping over it? The weather's fine; it's 'the glorious month of June,' we're in no hurry; why not take the magistrate at his word, and tramp east? I've often thought when I've been sweltering along on the old 96, and seen the tramps lying around under the trees smoking their pipes, and enjoying life, that the difference between my style of living and theirs — in the summertime, anyway — was mighty dearly paid for, by working three hundred and sixty-five days a year, for a soulless corporation. Somehow, it has always seemed to me that sometime I'd have a hack at it, and I don't suppose I'll ever have such a chance again. Nobody knows us here, so we needn't have any false modesty, and besides, it's a case of have to anyway. We've been ordered to turn tramp by a duly constituted authority, with a suitable penalty attached if we fail to obey; we haven't a red cent between us, so I don't see that there's any other way out of it. Come on! don't be so glum. There are thousands of tramps, and we look the part; so let's make the best of it, and get whatever fun out of it we can, — what do you say?"

I suppose the natural depravity that lies so near the surface in everybody's nature, responded to the appeal; for my spirits rose at once, and I said, "All right! I'm with you; but I'll tell you one thing, I won't beg. You'll have to do all that part of it."

"Who said anything about begging? Do you

remember that lead-pencil peddler that stopped at the boarding-house for a week last fall? He was an almighty wide-awake fellow. I got quite well acquainted with him, and he told me all about himself. I didn't believe all he said, but I'm satisfied that most of it was true. He said the man didn't live that he'd work for, no matter how good the job was, or the pay either. He said he had always made a good living, and been his own boss; and he told me how he and another fellow put in a whole summer, tramping from New York to Cleveland, Ohio. They never begged, and therefore they were never refused. Never you mind how it was done; I know, and that's enough."

We had taken to the New York Central Railroad, and were well out into the country, when it became dark, and in spite of my determination to enjoy the experience, a lonesome, half-scared feeling would come over me when I remembered that I had no money, and didn't know where I was going to sleep that night.

After walking — as it seemed to me — hours and hours, until my feet and legs ached so that it seemed as if I should drop, we sat down on the bank, to rest. As we had eaten nothing for more than twenty-four hours, I suggested that the sound of the dinner bell would be more than welcome. To this hint Frank replied, "Knights of the road, of our degree, that is, those who are too proud to beg, and too lazy to work, must do the other thing; that's why we travel so late. If I'm not mistaken, there's a farmhouse just round the curve, and as every man's hand is against us, I propose that our hand be against every man. The first thing to do is to provide ourselves with good serviceable cudgels, because the fool dogs that these farmers keep seldom know enough to mind their own business."

After we got our clubs cut and trimmed to suit, we reconnoitred the farmer's barn. It was the first time that I had ever been engaged in such a burglarious proceeding, and I was terribly frightened.

To go marauding about strange premises in the dark, not knowing what you will find on turning a corner or opening a door, but realizing that the owner would be perfectly justified in shooting you on sight, is not pleasant to a novice; but the faintness of incipient starvation made me, if not brave, at least desperate. We were in search of the hen-roost — a noble occupation for my father's son. Frank, as the leader of the forlorn hope, went ahead; while I brought up the rear, to look out for dogs and farmers. Fortunately for us there didn't seem to be any dogs, and the barn was so far from the house that our noiseless proceeding failed to disturb the peaceful slumbers of the honest man, who, tired from his day's work, was no doubt snoring lustily in peace, while we two scallywag tramps robbed him of the fruit of his honest toil.

Once Frank pulled open a door or shutter which was unexpectedly hinged at the bottom, and, before he could catch it, it dropped with a reverberating bang and rattle against the side of the building, making noise enough to alarm a county. Breathlessly and in hot haste we retreated to the railroad, and I was for abandoning the job altogether; but Frank strolled carelessly toward the house, and, having satisfied himself that no one was stirring, we resumed our operations. Frank assured me that, on the falling of the door he heard from within the building a startled clucking and rustling which told him that "Eureka" was the word.

He climbed through the hole, — no money could have tempted me to do that, — and presently I heard a whispered "Here!" and a Plymouth Rock hen with her head under her wing was passed out to me. I waited, expecting him to come out. It seemed an hour when I again saw a spot of extra blackness in the dark square and received a rooster. Frank soon followed, and, giving him the rooster, we got away from there at once. He had been all over the place, he told me, in search of eggs; but though he found none, he did find a lump of rock salt in a manger. It had probably been nosed over and licked by the horse for weeks, but that wouldn't hurt it any *inside*, would it?

We walked a good five miles before we dared to cook our game. In the meantime, we had wrung their necks, borrowed a ten-quart milking-pail that we saw inverted on top of a fence stake, and filled it with new potatoes and green onions. Coming to a bridge over a stream, we decided that no better place for breakfast could be found. There was an old wreck of a building close by which supplied us with ample fuel. We disembowelled our fowls, skinned them, and, without wasting even the heads, soon had them boiling merrily under the bridge, in company with the potatoes, onions, and a generous lump of salt. The light of our fire must have shone up through the ties and rails of the bridge, for several freight trains called for brakes, thinking, no doubt, that the bridge was on fire; and on discovering their mistake, they would pull out again, and go clanking and pounding over our heads, cursing us for the annoyance we had caused them. One fellow threw a shovelful of soft coal down upon us, a quart of which (estimated) went to the seasoning of our stew. But, as Frank remarked, while we could have got along without the additional ingredient, still he had heard it said that it was very nutritious, and as we had both, no doubt, swallowed many pounds of it during our railroad experience, we needn't mind a trifle more now; we could let the dish stand a bit, and the heaviest particles would sink. However, we always carried the pail to a sheltered place after that whenever a train was passing.

The odors that arose from that boiling pot will remain in my memory while life lasts, as the most delicious that I ever smelled. It was tantalizing to fish up a piece of meat with a pointed stick and find it tough yet, — beyond all hopes of mastication. It was getting daylight. Frank had remained for a bit seated on a stone behind me, watching the "killies" swimming in the shallow water, while I stirred the pot. I had just made an ineffectual attempt to bite the rooster's neck, when, *feeling* Frank standing at my back looking into the pot, I said, "I wonder how some of those killies would go in this mess?" "Oh, I don't know anything about *that*," said a strange voice, and, looking up, I found a robust, full-bearded young farmer watching me. I threw a hurried glance around for Frank; he was nowhere in sight. I wondered if he had been quietly nabbed and I was to be next. "Fine mornin'," said I, with all the composure — or effrontery, if you like — at my command. "Yes," said he; "the mornin's all right." But he never took his eyes off the pot, where, as I continued to stir, the hen's and rooster's heads circled round and round after each other in a merry race, encouraged and accompanied by crowds of enthusiastic partisans, in the shape of potatoes and onions, — the regatta taking place in a miniature reproduction of the Black Sea, due to the unsolicited contribution of soft coal. The situation was embarrassing. I felt the young stranger's presence to be *de trop*, his visit untimely, and wondered at his ill manners. Couldn't he see that we had not yet breakfasted?

While I was in this predicament, not wishing to be inhospitable, and yet — Frank appeared upon the scene with his club. I never could have believed that my chum, Frank Manly, the dashing young engineer, the adored of the girls, the central figure at all balls and picnics, the young man of whom I had often heard it said that even when he was firing, he could get off his engine at the end of a hundred and fifty mile run, looking as if he had just come from the hotel, — could ever look like this. His three days' growth of heavy red beard, the yellow and green tints of a rapidly disappearing black eye, a shiny crimson band across his nose and cheek bones, where he had been unaccountably sunburned the day before, together with his generally ragged and dirty appearance, had transformed him into as tough a looking specimen of the genus *tramp* as was ever seen, even on the comic opera stage. With the correct swagger and hoarseness of voice, he approached and asked, "How's that d—d swill gettin' along? Those d—d farmers around here ought ter be clubbed ter death fer the way they starve their poultry. I ain't had a decent meal since I left Syracuse. How's *your* hens, ol' man, hey?" and he gave the unoffending tiller of the soil a vicious dig in the ribs with the end of his cudgel that nearly doubled him up.

The farmer drew away a bit, and with a much more respectful air than he had used when he thought I was alone, said, "That old buildin' belongs to me, boys; I bought it from the railroad company; take what you want fer your fire, but don't burn the buildin' itself, will ye?"

"There, now!" said Frank; "I'm glad you told us that, because we thought it belonged to the railroad, and that's just what we were goin' to do to it—burn it up; but now, of course, we'll let it alone. Won't you have some breakfast with us, neighbor? It don't look quite as nice as it would if that d—d fireman hadn't dumped a scoopful of coal into it, but it's all the more filling, and just as healthy."

"No, thank ye; my breakfast's waiting for me up to the house."

"Didn't have manners enough to return the invitation, did he?" said Frank. "The first thing he'll do will be to count his chickens, and the next to send his hired man, if he's got one, or go himself if he hasn't, for the constable to arrest two tramps that are having a blow-out of boiled hen, down under the railroad bridge; so, of course, we've got to move out of the kitchen into the breakfast room. Come on!"

Shoving his club through the handle of the pail, I grasped the other end, and we moved our Lares and Penates, *not* along the track, — oh no, we were getting too wary for such work as that, — but down the bed of the stream, towards a small wood half a mile or so away, where, having arrived at last, we greedily devoured our long-delayed meal, the first to be eaten by us in the field. With pointed sticks we fished out the fragments of the dismembered fowls, and what we were unable to chew, we swallowed whole, taking alternate drinks from the pail, of the inky broth down to the very dregs; as the vegetables had all boiled to a mush, I have never been able to satisfy myself even to this day, that the major part of the coal contribution did not remain suspended in it. However, be that as it may, it was a most delicious and satisfying meal, although about one-third the quantity of salt would have been an improvement.

As we each contained a fully matured fowl, we now felt inclined to sleep, and the day being fine, we crawled into a clump of bushes, and slept the sleep that is known only to possessors of full stomachs and clear consciences.

I awoke about three o'clock in the afternoon lying on my back, with my mouth wide open, and so dry that I could not close it. Frank was in the same position, and looking down his throat, I saw that he too was completely burned out by the saline mess in his stomach. I took the pail down to the brook, and after taking the biggest drink that I ever remember, filled it, carried it back, and awoke Frank. When he saw me with the pail, he reached for it and drank, until I thought I would surely have to make a second trip, but he put it down at last, and said, "By George, I never lived so high in my life. I don't wonder tramps stick to their jobs as they do. Did you ever eat anything as good as that stew? I never did, and I never drank anything so good as that water, nor so much." We sat in the warm sun and talked, and drank water, Frank remarking that one of the beauties of tramping was that you didn't have to eat all the time, for after one such hearty meal as we had enjoyed you could live a couple of days on water.

We missed the comfort of a smoke; for though we each had a pipe and matches, we had no tobacco. Frank asked me what kind of a shot I was. I told him I hadn't fired a shot since Lee surrendered — a standard joke on the road, attributed to an intensely patriotic blacksmith in the shop, who was said to have been all through the war, and to have made the reply in a very dignified manner to some of the boys, who invited him to go on a hunting party. He asked me if I was a good hand at snipe-shooting, and said he would show me how it was done, the next time we came to a town.

Having sufficiently rested ourselves, we returned by a wide détour to the railroad, and resumed our easterly course. We tramped along silently for a while, when on glancing back, I saw a man coming after us at a rapid rate. My guilty conscience took alarm at once, and I asked Frank if he supposed it could be a constable after us, on account of our little irregularity of the previous evening. "Na-a!" said he, "and sposen it was, ain't we two to one? and what are these clubs for?" I didn't just like the reckless, defiant air that seemed to be growing upon him, although when I mentioned it, he assured me that it was from me that he had learned it. As the man was gaining rapidly on us, we waited for him to come up. He turned out to be a young fellow of twenty or thereabouts who had been working as a section hand on the Lehigh Valley road. He had been laid off, and hearing that a former employer had a contract to build some railroad in the neighborhood of Jersey City, this energetic young fellow had started on a walk of over four hundred and twenty miles on the bare possibility of getting employment, of the hardest kind, at a dollar, or a dollar and a quarter per day, *provided* the rumor proved to be true. He was the most energetic tramp that we ever saw. He gave us each a pipeful of tobacco and advised us to go with him, assuring us that he could get us a job on our arrival. But when we declined, he bid us good-day and started off again at a killing pace, saying that he intended to make forty miles per day, which, at the rate he was going, he could easily do if only he were able to keep it up.

CHAPTER XVI

THE MONOTONY OF THE TIES — THE USE OF MILK-PAILS — A KINDLY PROVIDENCE — SNIPE-SHOOTING — A DISCOVERY IN NATURAL HISTORY — HUNTING TURKEYS — HOP-PICKING — IN FUNDS AGAIN

Tiring of the monotony of the ties, we branched off into a country road. I, being in advance, saw a couple of half-grown roosters fighting just inside the fence. I reached in between the bars, and grasped the pair by their necks with one hand, as they were viciously but feebly pecking away at each other, like a pair of gamy but exhausted gladiators. The firm grip that I had on their necks prevented them from commenting on this summary method of restoring the peace.

The house being out of sight behind us, I held my kicking and flapping prey aloft for Frank's admiration. "Gosh!" said he, "broilers for tea! What better could anybody ask than that?" As they were inconsiderately scattering their tell-tale feathers about the place and over me, we quietly stretched their necks, and each taking one, were carelessly walking along looking for a good place to establish our kitchen, when it occurred to me that there was no necessity of making such a vainglorious display of our success, and I suggested to Frank that it would be as well to hide them under our coats.

None too soon, either; for we came directly upon a buggy containing three brawny farmers, who, we felt sure, would have interviewed us to our detriment, if they had seen the provisions.

Seeing signs of a town ahead of us, we determined to partake of our evening meal before entering; so we again took to the convenient woods, built a fire, and after having skinned and halved our birds, held them on sharpened sticks to the blaze.

The result could not be called altogether satisfactory. In the first place, the fire was so hot that it burned our hands and faces, so that we were unable to hold the meat in sufficiently close proximity to it long enough to cook it thoroughly, although we did succeed in getting it well smoked. "What fools we are," said Frank, "to stand over this fire and roast ourselves here. This is the way to do it; see?" and sharpening the end of his stick he stuck it in the ground in such a way that the half bird hung over near the flame. This was such an evident improvement, that we both hurried to cut other sticks, on which to impale the rest of our meat. But, alas, on returning to the kitchen, we found that an eddy of wind had caused the fire to burn our sticks off; and as the broils had disappeared, it was safe to infer that they had fallen into the fire.

A hasty scattering of the brands brought them to light, sadly scorched and withered, but as we soon found, juicy and raw within. A short consultation resulted in our getting sticks five or six feet long, for the next experiment, so that we could sit at a comfortable distance from the fire ourselves, and still retain control over the culinary operations. We squatted on our hunkers until we ached, holding the remainder of our provisions to the fire with one hand, like simple Simon fishing for the whale, while we gnawed alternate mouthfuls of cinder and raw chicken from the other.

By the time we had finished our repast, we were spitting ink, and unable to realize that we had dined; so we voted the broil a failure, and decided hereafter to stew our provisions. Not the least convincing argument which led to this decision, was the fact that rock salt when licked between mouthfuls, did not assimilate with the food as satisfactorily as when boiled with it, to say nothing of the flavor of vegetables and the filling qualities of water; and Frank sagely observed that as providence had so kindly impressed upon the minds of the New York farmers the desirability of leaving their milk-pails out of doors over night, we never need lack for cooking-utensils, or take the trouble to carry them with us.

As there was nothing to detain us longer in the woods, we started for the town, where Frank was desirous of arriving before dark, in order to initiate me into the noble sport of snipe-shooting, this exceedingly gamy fowl being most easily traced to its lair in daylight. "Oh, there's a fine one. See?" Yes, I saw a cigar butt. Frank stooped with an air of well-affected carelessness, as if to scratch his ankle, and "lifted" the snipe. We left town well stocked with a varied outfit of tobacco — Havana, Connecticut, North Carolina. We had all the brands.

We were not lucky that night in our search for shelter; and at last had recourse to a field filled with haycocks, under one of which we found most uncomfortable lodgings. The stubble underneath pricked us, and the damp, half-cured hay was unpleasant and inefficient as bed-clothes. During the night it rained, and after trying in vain to shelter ourselves with the hay until we were drenched, we left our inhospitable quarters, and tramped wearily and disconsolately along the track in single file, I grumbling at our ill-luck, and Frank, the philosopher, assuring me that as we were in the worst possible predicament now, the next change was bound to be for the better. And so it was; for there suddenly loomed up in front of us a vacant barn, or something, into which we crawled, and finding a dry corner, shivered and slept, slept and shivered, until daylight.

We were driven out by hunger, ravenous hunger, and made a discovery which was ever afterward of inestimable benefit to us. It was that in the early morning the barnyard fowls go a-field in search, I presume, of the proverbial early worm. In thus putting a respectable distance between themselves and the homestead, they confer a priceless boon upon such hungry wayfarers as have sworn to subsist solely on the fruit of the chase.

Another new and strange trait in the characters of these bipeds we discovered, which was, that when hunting in the long grass, they would not — as in all other cases — flee squawking towards home on our approach, but content themselves with merely squatting quietly in their tracks, whence we raised them in a loving embrace.

We never starved after that; for, though we did not restrict our hunting to this unexciting method, we depended on it when all else failed. I shall never forget the day when we made our first capture of half-grown turkeys. We came upon them in a field, — not a house nor a human being in sight; there must have been twenty-five or thirty of them — long-legged, long-necked, peeping Toms. It looked as though we could walk right in among them and pick them up, but that was a mistake; for though they didn't run off to any distance, they dodged, and fluttered, and peeped; and we ran after them, and fell down, until at last, exasperated, we fired our clubs at the bunches of them with force enough to have knocked down a house; and, somehow, the club would fly over their heads, or hit a stone and be deflected from its course, while they would huddle together in a scared crowd, and peep at us as we ran, red-faced and breathless, after our clubs again.

Of course, we succeeded at last; and, with a whole boiled turkey inside of each of us, together with the "fixin's," we enjoyed the sound sleep which is the invariable reward of honest and *successful* endeavor.

The turkeys were so luscious that we decided, hereafter, to dally no more with the robust physique of the maternal hen, as long as this year's turkeys were available. Three days we camped in the neighborhood, and infested that turkey-run; then, not wishing to outstay our welcome, we turned our faces again to the rising sun, each carrying a smoke-begrimed tin pail containing two dismembered young turkeys, preserved with the last of our salt pounded fine.

As our next meal must be eaten fresh, unless we could procure salt, we drew straws to decide who should beg that which we were unable to stea— levy.

I was elected, as I felt sure I should be, and, taking our only tankard (*anglicè*, tomato can), I sheepishly knocked at the door of the first house. A vixenish female shouted to me from within, to the effect that if I didn't clear out she would set "Tige" at me. I asked if she wouldn't please give me a little salt.

"Salt!" she shrieked; "for the land's sake, what do you want with salt? I never knew a tramp to come beggin' for salt, before. Yes, I'll give you all the salt you want. The Lord knows, I wish they wouldn't none of 'em ask for anything else but *salt.*"

So saying, and having relieved me of the embarrassing necessity of answering her first question by her own flow of volubility, she filled my can with salt; and thus ended my first and only experience in begging, of which I was, and am yet, heartily ashamed.

In order to show our gratitude to the lady, we gathered in fourteen ducklings which we found paddling in a little pond just out of sight of the house. They were insignificant little yellow balls of fluff, and, as we disdained to accept the parent duck, they served merely to thicken and flavor our soup.

I sometimes became discouraged, and wished that we might find a job somewhere; but Frank's light-heartedness never failed him, and it seemed especially to break out every little while at my expense. One day I awkwardly stubbed my toe, with the result that the sole of my shoe parted company with the upper, as far back as the instep. At this mishap, Frank — whose shoes remained strangely sound — laughed uproariously. As I was obliged to lift my foot high in the air, and bring it down with a scraping motion to prevent doubling the sole under me, I suppose that my gait was rather odd, but it seemed to me that I was entitled to sympathy from him; instead of which I got the jeering remark, "Ho! ho! you're done; you'll soon be barefoot now." I so forgot myself as to make a vicious swipe at him with my club, which he ducked, to be sure; but I had the satisfaction of seeing the top of his hat fly off, leaving him only the rim and sides.

This was exceedingly gratifying to me; for on account of Frank's neat and tidy habits, his clothing was in a much better state of preservation than mine.

No matter where we slept, in barn or box-car, he always laid his hat carefully at a safe distance; turned his coat inside out, folded it carefully, and laid it under his head; then on rising he would brush and shake his clothes, picking off every speck of hayseed or dirt, while I impatiently called him to come on. I usually laid my hat handy, so that in case we were disturbed I could be sure of finding it, with the invariable result, that I would lie on it during the night, — a treatment which a straw hat resents by becoming prematurely venerable in appearance, with its brim turned half a dozen different ways, and its crown a shapeless mass. I slept in my coat for the same reason, and as I had not the patience to go all over it the way he did, it not only became shapeless, but also very dirty. Hence I was well pleased to see his carefully preserved hat become at one fell blow more dilapidated even than mine.

The good-natured fellow only laughed at my rage and his own mishap, and set himself at once to sew the crown in again with a piece of tough grass; using the small blade of his knife for an awl. I found a piece of rusty wire and tied the sole of my shoe up the best way I could, but not being as handy as he, I made but a poor job of it, the wire continually coming off; while one would have had to look sharp to notice the repairs to his hat.

That afternoon we entered a small village, and spurred on by necessity, I entered a cobbler's shop, and asked for the loan of a few pegs to fasten my sole on with. The kindly German not only gave me pegs, but seeing that I was unable to do the job myself, he roughly pegged it on for me; for which I thanked him profusely at the time, and repeat it here now.

We avoided as much as possible associating with the fraternity. Sometimes we walked as hard as we could for a day or two, — why, we knew not, — then again we would loiter for days; resting our tired feet and absorbing ozone. One whole day we spent on top of a small hill, with a few pine trees growing about. The most of the day I occupied myself trying to kill an old woodchuck, who had a hole under a stump on the side of the hill. I would lie on my belly just above his hole, with a big rock and watch for him to come out; by and by I would see the tip of a gray snout where there had before been nothing but hole. I would not be able to perceive the slightest movement to it, and yet after a while I could see that it was farther out than before; slowly, imperceptibly, like the hour hand of a clock, it would emerge. When the entire head was in sight, I would cautiously raise my rock, only to see it disappear like a flash at the very first move I made. It must be terrible to have cultivated caution all one's life to such a degree that every sound, no matter how slight, should overwhelm one with the fear of death. I think I would rather be dead at once and have it over with.

It would be hours before the gray muzzle would

appear again; during all of which time I was obliged to lie so absolutely still that every bone in me ached, while innumerable creeping and buzzing things disported and regaled themselves at my expense. I soon learned that my only hope of success lay in having my rock poised ready when the time came, and so I held it aloft for ages, as it seemed, and wished that he would come out, and sympathized with Saint Simon Stylites; and when at last the auspicious moment arrived, I was so stiff and cramped that the rock didn't hit within a foot of the hole, and wouldn't have hit him if it had; for he was too quick. I wanted that woodchuck awfully that afternoon, for I had heard, when a boy, that they made a splendid roast; so I was terribly disappointed, when at last I had to acknowledge that I must give up. I have since learned that they are not nice; so I don't care anything about it now.

As we meandered gently along the great steel highway, we heard from some of the riff-raff whom we met — or more frequently who overtook and passed us — fairy-like tales of the pleasures and profits of hop-picking. So hoping to be able to enjoy ourselves, and at the same time earn the wherewithal to replenish our dilapidated wardrobes, we said that we would pick hops — provided we reached the hop country in time. Shortly after coming to this conclusion, we were hailed one day by a big, clean, wholesome-looking young German with: "Say, you fellers don' look like regly tramps; do you vant to vork?" "Yes," said I, hastily, thinking of my weak shoe, and some other things.

"Vell, all thright! I gif you tventy dollers de mont, and board, to thravel mit a dhrashin machine; vat you say?" Before I could get my mouth open, Frank blurted out, "Naw, it's too hard work — we're hop-pickers."

"So-o? I guess you fellers don' vants to vork vera mooch; you are notting else as regly thramps; dat's betther you look out for dem bolicemons; I dell you he make you vork."

I was so mad I could hardly keep from taking another crack at Frank's hat; twenty dollars a month and grub! a fortune within our grasp! But he said he had heard of those threshing-machine jobs before. He said they never hired anybody but tramps; worked them eighteen hours per day, starved them to death, and then refused to pay; sometimes even having them arrested on a false charge of thieving.

From the Syracuse salt pans we replenished our stock of salt, breaking off the long "icicles" that formed wherever there was a slight leak, and as I became worried for fear we should be late at the hop-fields, we stowed ourselves away in the feed-trough of an empty "palace horse car," and rode to Oneida, where we saw the — to us — strange and disenchanting sight of women in bloomers; from here we took a day's march down into Madison County where the hops grow. We had heard in Oneida that the hop crop was heavy, and that pickers were not offering themselves in very great quantities, so we were emboldened to strike the owner of a flourishing hop-yard for a job. He hemmed and hawed, said he usually engaged his pickers in advance; but admitted that this season he hadn't attended to it. This was our cue, and we expatiated on the scarcity of pickers; we had come directly from Oneida and knew whereof we spoke. He eyed us suspiciously, — our appearance was certainly not prepossessing, — and then remarked that this was only Thursday, and he wasn't going to begin until Monday. But we assured him that he had better secure us now or he would regret it. We promised to work for our board in the meantime; but he said that there were only two more working days, and then he would have to keep us over Sunday for nothing. Our eloquence finally prevailed over his mercenary scruples, and he set us to the time-honored tramp's employment of sawing wood. We had eaten nothing that day, and as we bent our backs to the unfamiliar work, we perspired, and felt dizzy and faint.

As it was late in the afternoon, we buoyed up our hopes with the thoughts of the good farmhouse supper we were to get later on; and seeing several immense cans near the barnyard, we revelled expectantly in the luxury of oceans of bread and milk, new milk fresh from the cow.

When it began to get dark, the hands drove up a large herd of cows, and from where we slaved on our empty stomachs we could dimly see them emerge, one after another, and pour the contents of their milk-pails into the big cans, which they had previously loaded on a wagon. I could stand it no longer, so, dropping my saw, I said to Frank, "I'm going to have a drink of milk if the whole road stops." As I neared the wagon, a big, good-natured-looking countryman approached it from the other side; and I said, "Hey, Johnny! give us a drink of milk, will ye?"

He stared at me a moment, then emptying his pail where so many had preceded it, thumbed his nose at me, and said in that aggravating, smarty way, that such people frequently have, "No, sirree; thet milk's for the cheese factory, not for tramps." And there were barrels of it.

At last, when the cows were milked, the chores all done, and it was too dark to see anything, the "help," after noisily washing themselves at a rainwater barrel, and bragging in loud voices — for the farmer's benefit — about how much work they had done, and how much they could do, blundered clumsily into the house.

"Well, blast them!" said Frank; "I wonder if they don't intend to call us to supper. I've a great mind to collar a couple of his chickens, and a pail of that milk they're so almighty stingy with, and clear out." Just then the tall, gaunt form of the farmer appeared in the door, and he sung out, "Hey, you two men, come in an' eat."

"I should think he was calling his hogs," said

Frank, — "'come in an' eat!'" However, our indignation did not prevent us from responding with alacrity to the summons.

A pan of *cold* boiled potatoes, with their jackets on, and a four-pound piece of cold boiled salt pork, all fat, and a loaf of bread that might have been one of the foundation bricks of the tower of Babel, — this, and nothing more, was the evening meal spread by this wealthy farmer of the Empire State for himself, his family, and his help. No, I do the good man an injustice; there was a big white pitcher of well water, cold and sparkling, to be sure, but with the flavor of all his Dutch ancestors pervading it. Afterwards, when from long residence I acquired the privilege of being familiar with the help, I asked one of them if they ever cleaned out the well. He answered by asking, "What fer?"

I am not, and never was, "partial" to fat salt pork; neither was Frank. That night as we composed ourselves to sleep in the hop-kiln, Frank asked me how I liked hop-picking as far as I had got. I told him not to be discouraged; I said that we had accomplished something anyway, for instead of tramps, we were now "honest workingmen." On Monday the hop-pickers arrived, and a busy scene at once ensued. The farmer put on his store clothes and developed at once into a "boss." He was even too dignified to superintend the work himself. There was one man who was boss of the whole outfit, like a general superintendent, and then there were division superintendents under him, called "pole-pullers." They were pretty big men in their small way. Although the experienced pickers feared them not, yet to strangers, and tough-looking strangers like Frank and me, they were offensively pompous. As Sancho Panza said when eulogizing his master, they were "humble with the haughty, and haughty with the humble." They said that we put too many leaves in with our hops, and kicked because we were so long filling our boxes, although the Lord knows we were anxious enough to fill them quickly; for the longer you are about it, the more you have to put in, as they wilt so fast, and being paid by the box, a slow picker is obliged to pick many more hops for the same amount of money than a rapid one is. The old timers, pretty girls, and fast pickers, can cajole the pole-puller into bringing them *good* poles, *i.e.* those on which the hops grow in big, thick clusters, so that they can be scraped off by the handful, rapidly filling the box; while the unfortunates who are without influence must take the measly ones, on which leaves predominate. Needless to say, Frank and I were in the latter class, so we stood there and picked, and sweated, and labored like galley slaves, to fill the apparently bottomless box; while the others, being acquainted and *respectable*, chatted, laughed, and sang songs all day, thereby grievously emphasizing our Ishmaelitish condition. In the evening they met at different hop-yards, as they were called, and passed the time dancing and enjoying themselves.

At these merrymakings we were allowed to look on.

With the arrival of the hop-pickers, our fare suddenly and wonderfully improved, for no man dare feed his pickers poorly; if he did, he would get none the next season. It is the only "trade" that I know of where the operatives are so independent. How we two hungry tramps did cover ourselves with glory at the table. We would be the first to sit down, and would shovel away for dear life, until the last picker had returned to work, and then for shame's sake we had to leave the table still hungry; and though we kept it up during our stay, we never succeeded in filling that long-felt want.

As it is one of the axioms of hop-picking that in the cool of the morning, while the dew is still on the hops, they wilt less rapidly than later on, and therefore the boxes can be more quickly filled, the ethics of the trade require early rising. And the same being true of the evening, the frugal pickers put in an outrageously long day, for pay at which an Italian laborer would turn up his patrician nose. On the first Saturday night, we lined up with the rest, and presenting our tickets which had been punched by the pole-puller during the week, to show the number of "hop-sacks" we had filled, received our pay, or rather, to simplify the transaction, I presented both tickets and received the money.

That evening we went to the store and bought smoking-tobacco, pipes, matches, and *socks*. How good it was to smoke tobacco at first hand once more, and to wear socks with feet to them, instead of the hollow mockeries which we had been wearing now for some time, and which required constant watching to prevent them soaring above the tops of our shoes, and revealing our poverty-stricken makeshifts to an unsympathetic world!

How Frank managed it, I don't know; but on the following Sunday he borrowed shaving-tools from one of the hands, and took off the villanous looking red stubble that had so long disfigured him. I never had noticed before that he was particularly good looking, so that I was surprised to see how handsome he was, and treated myself to the same luxury, with the extremely gratifying result that one of the Oneida belles actually smiled on me, — or at me, — and that night I dreamed dreams.

CHAPTER XVII

GOOD-BYE TO HOP-PICKING — THE INDUSTRIAL FEVER — WE STEAL A RIDE — THE IMPERIOUS BRAKEMAN — SUBSISTING AGAIN ON THE ENEMY'S COUNTRY — TEN DAYS IN JAIL — MUCH NEEDED REST — HIRED AT LAST — AT THE THROTTLE AGAIN

We, being two of the poorest pickers, were the first to be discharged. The farmer let us stay over night, and gave us our breakfasts next morning, for which act of Christian charity I hereby return thanks. Perhaps he wished to give us the opportunity to put a day's march between ourselves and his farm before dark. Cheerily we took to the highway again. It was a beautiful summer's morning, and our spirits rose with the genial surroundings, until I, mistaking the cause of our hilarity, asked Frank if he didn't think it made a person feel happy and independent to have money in his pocket.

He looked off up the road, gave a queer smile, and said, "I dunno." It was the only allusion he ever made to the fact that I had constituted myself the treasurer of the concern. However, I didn't let on that I noticed; and as we shortly came in sight of another hop-yard, we applied for work,

Roundhouse Studies. — p. 266.

and, to our surprise, were hired at once, and at a slightly advanced rate of pay, too. We stayed a week in this place; and then, the season being over, we rose from our dormitory in the barn bright and early, seized two pairs of pullets, whose roosting-place we had noted the night before, confiscated the necessary milk-pail; and having laid in a supply of vegetables,—also from our late employer's garden, —we withdrew to a near-by sylvan dell, and breakfasted. But after the recent festivities our primitive cooking palled on my pampered palate, and I declared in favor of a job, wages, and a boarding-house. To all of which Frank gave a ready assent. With this determination to quit at the earliest opportunity the ancient and honorable order misnamed "Sons of Rest," we once more entered the highway, I, for one, sincerely hoping that here might end the trail of bones and feathers that had so far marked our course across the Empire State. We met a typical wanderer, who turned up his nose at us, when we told him that we had been picking hops. He said that he was going to the Oneida Community to get a job husking corn, and advised us to come along, saying that it paid better than hop-picking, which he contemptuously referred to as a "bum job."

The industrial fever being strong upon us, we agreed, and before nightfall had been refused employment, with suspicious glances, and curt speech, by the superintendent of the cannery. Once more we were obliged to pursue military tactics, and subsist upon the enemy's country.

The next day we fitted ourselves out with cheap cotton trousers, straw hats, and cowhide shoes. We also bought two cheap shirts each, experience having taught us that the clothes-lines of the country were an unreliable source on which to depend for underwear, the native women having a custom which cannot be too strongly deprecated, of taking in the wash before dark. We treated ourselves to a restaurant dinner, and then, not having money enough left to amount to anything, we bought a bag of salt; and feeling the need of stimulant after our hard season's labor, we spent the very modest remainder in beer, and for a brief hour or so we knew the elation of spirit and freedom from carking care that a moderate indulgence in this mild form of alcohol produces.

That night found us snugly ensconced in the corner of an empty box-car, en route for the effete east. If it is true that "westward the tide of empire takes its way," then indeed was ours a retrograde movement. If any person had asked us where we were going, we could not have told him; all we knew was that we wanted a job. And while every freight train on every railroad in the country was taking homeless, unemployed men — tramps — from the overcrowded east to the great and growing west in search of a place where their labor would purchase for them that which nature furnishes in abundance to every living thing but man, — food and shelter, — we two, who had sat for years on the right side of locomotives, — the master spirits of moving trains, — squeezed ourselves tightly into the corner of an old-box car, to evade the glance of the imperious brakeman who had looked in while the train stood at the water-plug, that we might go east.

Before we slept, we had decided that the only thing left for us was to seek employment of the lowest grade, — pick and shovel work. Why, I don't know, unless it was that we were influenced by our environment. Certainly we didn't look to be fit for anything else, and so I suppose we didn't feel that we were.

For a week we passed through an experience that was both humiliating and abusive. Brakemen, becoming exasperated when we told them that we had no money, flung us headlong from rapidly moving trains. City and village policemen ordered us to keep moving until we should be clear of their territory. Even the ducks by the roadside insulted our galled feet and weary limbs by admonishing us, in all seriousness, to "wa'k, wa'k, wa'k!" "Well, blast ye, ain't we walkin'?" said Frank. Once, while standing on a bridge and looking down at the railroad yard in Dewitt, a very black, ragged, and filthy negro touched me on the shoulder and said kindly, but with an air of freedom and equality that profoundly impressed me with my degradation:

"Hey, Johnny! yer better go som'er's 'n' pick de hayseed off'n yer clo'es; if dese yer railroad detectives sees yer, dey'll run yer in, fer suah, 'n' yer'll git a month in de cooler."

It was true we had slept in a barn that night; and while Frank, with his usual neatness, had carefully shaken and picked all the hayseed from his clothes, the telltales had marked me, even to this negro tramp, as a member of the order.

All these disagreeable incidents tended to disgust us more and more with our condition; but although we faithfully asked for employment at every place where there seemed the slightest prospect that it might be obtained, the fates, aided no doubt by our disreputable appearance, were against us, and our proffered services were coldly declined. At last, that which we had dreaded in an indefinable way for some time came to pass. We were bathing in the Mohawk one day, — a daily practice which we had adopted for sanitary reasons, — when a slab-sided individual appeared on the bank and ordered us to come ashore and get into our clothes "mighty quick!" As we had acquired somewhat of the spirit of the characters that we were personating, we recommended him to retire to a certain place which could hardly be considered a desirable locality in which to spend a summer outing. As he continued to annoy us by his ranting, we, being two, assailed him with volleys of wet stones, driving him from the vicinity of our clothes.

We came out then and dressed ourselves just in time to fall victims to our late tormentor and two other pumpkin-huskers that he had recruited from somewhere. We asked why we were arrested, and he told us that we would find out soon enough, advising us solemnly that anything that we might say would be used against us.

As our captors were ostentatiously armed with bludgeons of green birch while we had nothing, we concluded that discretion was the better part of valor, and went with them as meekly as we could to a considerable town some three miles farther on, where we were run into a lock-up, and kept until the next day on a diet of tepid water. We were then arraigned before some kind of an official, charged with vagrancy, disturbing the peace, and resisting an officer in the discharge of his duty.

We were found guilty on all three counts of the indictment, and sentenced to ten days in jail, — a mild punishment when you consider the heinousness of the crime.

We got a good and much-needed rest in the little jail. We were well fed, and required only to keep our premises clean and in order, so that really it was more an act of charity than of discipline; but the feeling that we had now received the highest degree in trampdom was not exhilarating, though even from this condition light-hearted Frank drew a grain of comfort; for he said that, having reached the very bottom of the ladder, our next change *must* be for the better. For my part, I could see no assurance that there was to be any change; I was under the impression that tramps regularly alternated between begging, stealing, and *jailing*. However, Frank was nearer right than either of us would have believed at the time. When our term expired, we were once more turned loose to prey upon the barnyards of the natives, but with a severe admonition to get out of town as fast as we knew how, or we might expect another and longer term of entertainment at the county's expense.

With this dire threat ringing in our ears, we proceeded to the outskirts of the place, and lay in wait near a convenient water-plug all day. In the evening we boarded an east-bound freight, and after sleeping soundly all night, awoke to find ourselves stationary in a small siding. A few moments' observation showed that we had been riding in a hay-car, and it had been left here near a cross-road for the convenience of the neighboring farmers, who probably had hay to ship. Thinking that we might find work here, as from what we could see of the country and buildings it appeared to be a land of well-to-do people, we started off down the cross-road, and after catching, cooking, and eating a hearty breakfast, we applied for employment to a well-dressed old gentleman whom we met riding a handsome horse.

"What can you do?" said he, stopping and looking at us with an interest so new to us, that it caused us no little apprehension. Scenting a job, we both together answered eagerly, "Anything."

"Well, but I mean, what have you done? have you any trade, or calling? is there any one thing that you can do better than another?"

We told him that we had no trade.

"Oh, I see," said he, with a rather supercilious smile, "just common tramps!"

The expression, and the way in which he said it cut me, and I answered, "No, sir, we are *not* common tramps; we never tramped until this summer, and wouldn't now if we could get anything to do. We're railroad men out of a job."

"If you're railroad men, why don't you go over back here where they're building that new road? I understand that the contractor wants all the help he can get."

"Where?" said we both, in a breath. He directed us, and off we went in hot haste, elated at the prospect of employment. Within half a mile from where we met the old gentleman we came upon a busy scene. They were building the roadbed of a double-track railroad, and in order to conciliate the residents, employment was given to all the men, boys, and draught animals who applied. There were horses, mules, and oxen, hauling dirt and stone in all manner of vehicles. Besides the native contingent, there were gangs of Italians, Swedes, and Germans, shovelling away for dear life, each gang presided over by an Irish foreman, who yelled at the laborers continually, while a big, black-whiskered man with a red face — the contractor — yelled at the foremen in turn. He saw us almost as soon as we did him, and beckoning to us, roared out, "What in h— are you fellers loafin' round for? Want a job?"

"Yes, sir."

"Hey, Mike! here's two good men fer ye; give 'em a couple of shovels an' let 'em git at that bank."

Hired at last, thank the Lord! Here was work enough for months. It was hard work in the blazing hot sun; our backs ached, and our hands were terribly blistered. Mike, our foreman, was a driver, whom nobody could do enough to suit; he was abusive too, but we didn't care, it was work. There were wages and meals and shelter attached to it, and that was what we were after. I never felt so proud as I did when I quit at six o'clock that night, and took my place at the long board table in the shanty to help eat the bountiful supper that contractor Gallagher furnished us. I was tired to death; every bone in me ached; but I had an appetite like an ostrich, and I was no longer a tramp. It was refreshing to hear the men talk. We were put into a gang of Swedes who could all talk English, and their conversation was not of tramping; for they had never been tramps, never expected to be, and, in fact, didn't seem to know that such people existed; and Frank and I took precious good care not to introduce the subject.

We learned that the pay was a dollar a day and

board. It seemed as if a diamond mine had opened at our feet; we began to build castles at once, — what could we not buy in a few months at that rate? A vista of wealth opened before us such as we had never dreamed of before. A dollar a day and board, nothing to pay out of our wages, only once in a while a suit of overclothes to work in! We marvelled at the contractor's liberality.

For two months we slaved under Mike Callahan's tyrannical rule; the road was pushed rapidly along through the nearly level farm land, and we were a long way from the place where we had been hired. We two were so overjoyed to be at work again, that we labored with a will. Occasionally, we had an opportunity to display our mechanical knowledge and skill, so that Mr. Callahan had come to depend on us when any unhandy or difficult job confronted him; therefore, when Mr. Gallagher rode up in his buggy one day and told Mike to send his two best men down to the village in the morning with their "kits," we were chosen.

Here we found half a dozen others, who had been drafted from the various gangs, and we learned that we were to go back down the road and assist in track-laying.

It was a little higher grade of work, so our pay was raised twenty-five cents per day — more wealth!

As fast as we got the ties and rails spiked, a little old locomotive hauled the flat cars on to them; the men shovelled the gravel off, the roadbed was graded, and the ties tamped. When we first went down there, the engine hauled eight or ten loaded cars, but gradually the engineer — a young fellow eighteen or twenty years of age — began to kick. He said that the engine was overloaded, — and so she was, — and he wanted a fireman. Gallagher said the engine had always hauled twelve cars before, and he didn't believe that the engineer knew his business. As for a fireman, he'd see him d—d first. Nearly every day Gallagher came to the job and had a row with the engineer, while the engine was getting worse and worse; until, at last, she stalled dead with eight cars, on a little knoll, with Gallagher looking right at her.

He was furious; he jumped on the engine, and hauled the young engineer out of the cab, kicked and beat him unmercifully; and finally told him that if he didn't clear out he would have him locked up. The young fellow wiped the blood and dirt from his face and demanded his money. At this, Gallagher had another fit, but contented himself with cursing the man, and telling him how much unnecessary expense he had put him to by reason of his incompetency. "And now," said Gallagher, "where in h— am I to get an engineer? Here 'tis three o'clock, Saturday; I'll have to lose the rest of this day, anyhow, and will be mighty lucky if I'm able to work Monday; for even if I get a man, I suppose you've hoodooed the engine so that she won't be good for nothin'."

After having relieved himself somewhat, he paid the man off, to get rid of him; and, as he was stepping into his buggy, I walked up to him, and said, "Mr. Gallagher, if you want an engineer, I'd like to have the job."

He was interested at once. "Are you an engineer?" said he.

"Yes, sir;" said I. "Both my friend and myself are locomotive engineers of several years' experience."

"By G—d, I believe it; you look like it. Why didn't you say so long ago? That d—d fool has had the life worried out of me. Well, now, I'll tell you what you do: it's no use starting up again, now the men are all knocked off; but you look that engine over, get acquainted with her, run her up and down the track here, if you like, this afternoon, and be ready to start to work Monday morning."

"Didn't you say that she used to haul twelve cars?"

"Yes; an' she did, too."

"Well, if you'll give me what I want, I'll guarantee to haul them, every day I work here, up any grade that I have seen on the road, so far."

"What do you want?"

"I want four men, besides myself, to work on that engine all day to-morrow, and I want a fireman; I won't run without a fireman."

"Want a job for that red-headed fellow, hey?"

"Yes, sir."

"Well, all right. Now I'll tell you what I'll do.

You tell Mullins to give you all the men you want, and pick them out yourself. Use everything you can get hold of round here, and put that engine in the best shape you can. Then if you can take twelve loads up Apple Tree grade Monday morning, I'll give you seventy-five dollars a month, and give Red-head fifty to fire for you; but if you don't take but ten, I'll only give you fifty dollars, and Red-head stays in the gang. What do you say to that?"

"I say all right," said I. "I'm perfectly satisfied."

I got my four men from Mullins, the foreman, and went at her at once. First, I took her down to a piece of straight track. Frank and I uncapped the steam-chests, and while the other two fellows pinched her for us, we set the valves a blamed sight nearer than they were before — they needed facing badly, but we had neither time nor tools. Then we took the cylinder-heads off, and set the packing-rings out so that they would touch the cylinders once in a while, anyhow; and then it was time to knock off for supper.

The next day we washed out the boiler, bored the tubes, repaired the arch and grate bars as well as we could, with what we could pick up around the place, and also opened the front end, cleaned out the nozzles and spark-netting, squared the diaphragm, set it where we thought it would be about right, picked up the blower-pipe which was lying there loose, and connected it, cut off an extra two feet that my predecessor had added to the stack in the vain effort to make her steam, and having filled the boiler, we set our two helpers at work firing up, while Frank and I amused ourselves taking up lost motion.

Having got steam, Frank banked the fire. I wouldn't move her until Monday morning. Mr. Gallagher was on hand bright and early, but he never came near the engine, or even looked at her. Frank pulled the fire down while I oiled, and I told him to notify me quietly when he was ready.

We backed up, and I told the men to couple on sixteen cars. The fellow who acted as a sort of conductor laughed at me; but I insisted, and she walked them up to the top of Apple Tree grade like a lady — blowing off the instant that I closed the throttle. I managed to steal a glance at Gallagher, and saw him turn with a grin and say something to the foreman, but he never came near the engine. He stayed round there for an hour or so, and then climbed into his buggy and rode off.

It was a week before I had an opportunity to speak to him, then he came up to the engine and asked how I was making out. I told him all right; and he said that he was satisfied if I was.

I ran and Frank fired the engine for Gallagher for four months. It was hard, dirty work, for it was our normal condition to be off the track. There was a great deal of rain that season and the sand-pit track was forever sliding from under us, to say nothing of the soft fills that we built out on the road, and then tried to haul heavily loaded gravel trains over. The natural consequence was that we spent most of our time on our backs in the mud, blocking up wheels and tracks. Then after the day's work of twelve or fourteen hours was done, we had our engine to take care of, and in the morning we had to be at work at least an hour before the rest, so as to be ready. However, we were happy, and as we had no chance to spend our money, we accepted the offer of Mr. Gallagher to leave it in his hands, for which he agreed to pay us six per cent interest. We became so stingy that we cut our living expenses down to the last possible cent, for we wished to have a good stake when the job was done, one experience of tramping being enough.

CHAPTER XVIII

BUNCOED BY GALLAGHER — AN OLD FRIEND TO THE RESCUE — PRACTICAL RAILROAD KNOWLEDGE — BUILDING UP A ROAD — A SUNDAY-SCHOOL EXCURSION — DISASTER — I LOSE MY NERVE — BECOME CONDUCTOR — A DRUNKEN ENGINEER

AFTER about four months of this kind of thing, Mullins came to the engine one morning and told us that he should not want her that day; he said that we might have a holiday. I asked him why, but he merely shrugged his shoulders and walked off.

Frank banked his fire, and we returned to the shanty, where we found the men standing about in groups, smoking their pipes and speculating on the cause of the stoppage of the work. Some of them, old railroad-builders, didn't hesitate to say openly that Gallagher had "busted up," or "was playing a sharp trick."

The latter proved to be the case, for we never saw him again, nor a cent of the four months' pay for which we had worked so hard. It was very discouraging. We didn't know what to do. We had no money, and were worse off for clothes than we had been when tramping, for all we had now were the dirty, ragged overalls in which we worked. Three days we hung around waiting for something to turn up, for all sorts of rumors were afloat. We heard that Gallagher had committed suicide, that he was in jail, and that he was coming back to pay all hands and start up the work again; the truth being that he had collared all the money he could lay his hands on and gone to Europe.

As it was agreed that somebody would have to finish the road, we decided — partly because we could not do otherwise — to wait developments, and try and get employment with the new man, resolving, however, never again to leave our wages in our employer's hands any longer than we were absolutely obliged to. Now that so many of us had been swindled out of our money, it occurred simultaneously to everybody that we might have known that there was something wrong when a big contractor like Gallagher borrowed money from his employees.

On the fourth morning after the collapse, a man nailed a notice on the side of the shanty, notifying all the late employees of the contractor who wished to enter the employ of the —— R. R. Co., to report at 10 A.M. to Mr. —— in the hotel at the village.

This Mr. —— proved to be our old general manager in Chicago, the kindly, genial old gentleman who was displaced when the new, hungry, bean-eating, down-east president got control of the road. He knew Frank and me at once, and said he was pleased to meet us. After making arrangements to have the work started up again immediately, he told us that the company owning the road had decided to finish it themselves; he said that he had been sent to superintend the construction, with orders to hire as many of the contractor's men as chose to work for the company, with the understanding that the railroad company would not be accountable for any wages due the men from the contractor.

He told Frank and me that he believed it was going to be a good road. He said they had millions of English capital behind them, and that his orders were, to have all the work done in a strictly first-class manner, no skimping on account of expense. He said that he had been appointed superintendent of construction, and would undoubtedly be superintendent of the road when completed; and he promised us that if we chose to stay with him he would see that we were properly taken care of. All of which you may be sure raised our spirits from the slough of despond to the seventh heaven of delight; for of permanent employment we had never dreamed while working for Gallagher, so that in reality his absconding with our four months' pay turned out to be a blessing in disguise. Frank improved the opportunity to remind me that he had predicted when we were in jail, that our next change would be for the better, and I was obliged to admit that it had indeed been the turning-point in our fortunes, for they had steadily improved from that day.

We now saw the practical side of Mr. ———'s railroad knowledge. In Chicago we had known him only as the gentlemanly general manager, seated in his luxurious office, and surrounded by obsequious clerks and stenographers.

Now we saw him, although a man over sixty years of age, equipped in long boots and rubber coat, floundering round in the mud; lugging ties, blocks or heavy wire switch ropes, and helping both by his knowledge and manual labor, to put cars and engine on the track.

He worked earlier and later than any other man on the job, and introduced new methods whereby the work was greatly expedited. Inside of a week he had a steam shovel at work in the gravel pit, and plough cars on the road. Within a month two brand-new passenger locomotives with the name of the road in gold letters on their tenders arrived, and Frank and I each took one, while our old engine was given to another man.

Mr. —— rode with me a great deal on the engine, and I learned to know him well, and to admire him sincerely. He told me that the incitement of the strike, and subsequent wrecking of the road in Chicago, was a stock-jobbing scheme inaugurated by the eastern syndicate which had secured control, and against whom he had fought as long as he could, but when they finally got control of enough shares of stock to elect their president, he didn't wait to be kicked out, but resigned.

Under the new management the road grew like a weed. The first division was opened for passenger traffic the next summer, and with my engine newly painted, and engine and train gayly decorated with flags, I had the pleasure of earning the first dollar for the company; which hangs in a gold frame in the president's private office to this day.

The road was a success from its inception; it became at once a favorite passenger route to the west, on account of its palatial cars, fine roadbed, magnificent scenery, and faultless service. I, being the senior engineer, chose the Chicago limited for my train, and Frank being second, took the other side of it, so that we were still closely connected; running the same engine on alternate days. It now seemed as if our troubles were indeed over. We had the most desirable train on a trunk line railroad, were intimate personal friends of the general superintendent, and our lines were indeed fallen in pleasant places.

Being prosperous, and no longer boys, we looked about among the numerous, handsome, and eligible young ladies of our acquaintance, and soon discovered that there was a certain one peculiarly adapted to each of us, and the natural consequence of this discovery was that we were both married within three months of each other. We bought adjoining lots, and erected handsome houses; each in every respect the duplicate of the other. Fortunately our wives had been life-long friends before their marriage, so that the most perfect harmony existed between the two families.

Three years after my marriage, having completed the payments on my house, I felt that I was entitled to a holiday; and as I had not heard from home for a number of years, I obtained ten days' leave of absence, and with my wife and boy revisited the scenes of my childhood.

Coal and iron having been discovered in the neighborhood, blast furnaces had been established, and that which I had left a quiet, peaceful country village, had become a grimy, smoky, thriving town.

I learned that my father had been dead seven years; my sisters were married, the elder having gone with her husband to California; while the younger was the wife of the superintendent of a large steel mill, recently erected in a neighboring town, which had grown up since I left home, on the site of a sheep pasture. Mother was living in the old homestead, hale and hearty, and was delighted to see her boy, as she called me, once more. She took to my wife right away, and my boy would have owned her body and soul in another week. But the railroad man is as much a slave to duty as is the soldier, and so my leave having expired, we regretfully bade the dear old mother adieu, after exacting a promise that she should come to us at Thanksgiving time, and returned.

Once more with hand on throttle, and head out of window, I went spinning over the iron on old 32, the most faithful engine that I ever knew. We both took great pride and comfort in her, and our train was of sufficient importance, and what was more yet, our acquaintance with the general superintendent was so intimate and so well known, that the master mechanic and round-house foreman were in the habit of doing pretty nearly all the work that either of us reported. I had noticed that the flanges on the leading engine truck wheels were getting worn pretty thin and sharp, and had spoken to the foreman about turning the truck round, so as to bring the good wheels ahead. He had promised to do so, but as I suppose he didn't consider it a matter of immediate importance, he let it go a week. I then asked Frank to report it, and he told me that he had done so before I did. I let it run for another week, and then as I didn't consider the engine to be quite safe with them, I told the foreman that I should have to go to the master mechanic about it, if he didn't attend to it right away.

"All right," said he, "I'll surely do it next trip in. I've been so busy for the last couple of weeks that I couldn't possibly spare a man a minute for any purpose."

"Very well," said I; "I'll take her out this trip; but I won't take her out again until that truck's turned round; 'tain't safe."

A heavy Sunday-school excursion train left half an hour ahead of me. As she was an extra, I had no occasion to look out for her; it was her business to keep out of my way. They had ten cars, every seat filled, mostly women and children. The ferry boat was ten minutes late, and as our time had been shortened up fifteen minutes on the last time table, I knew I would have hard work to get in on time. So as soon as I got clear of the yard I let the old girl go for all there was in her, working all the fine points known to engineers to get every ounce of speed out of her, and yet keep her in steam, fire, and water. Eight miles out there was a low ridge over which the road ran; it was a short, rather steep grade up, and then a long gentle sweep down for about two miles, around a curve, and then fairly level running ground for the next twenty-five miles. When she pitched over the top of the knoll, I started down the long grade at a good gait, for here was my chance to get a swing on to carry me over the long level stretch beyond the curve.

As she gathered headway, I hooked her back a notch at a time, until she was flying like a comet. The cars rolled like logs in a lake, and as I glanced back, the last two were entirely obscured by the dense cloud of dust that we tore up from the track as we sped along. She was going sixty-five miles per hour if she was an inch. The sensation was exhilarating. I know of nothing that will fill a man with such a sense of joyful mastery as to sit at the head of a fast-flying train, a record-breaking train, and realize that it is his work, that there is no higher authority than himself here; the superintendent, general manager, and president are left behind, and he alone is boss and king. As I approached the curve I could see that the excursion train was in the switch just beyond, waiting for me. I blew a crossing signal to let them know that I was coming, because excursionists have a great habit of getting off and spreading themselves all over creation every time their train stops, and I didn't wish to kill any of them. I fancied I could hear the women and children utter little frightened screeches as we flew by them.

It was a long, easy curve, and yet the speed was such that she struck it as solidly as if it had been a brick wall; she tossed her head round for an instant, and then plunged straight into the side of that ten-car train crammed full of happy women and children.

The flange of the leading wheel on the engine truck had broken, and allowed the engine to leave the track. Naturally, as she tore the rails from the ties in her mad flight, the whole train followed her. The engine crashed diagonally through four cars, smashing them as effectually as you could smash the same number of eggs with an axe. The cars following, rammed, telescoped, and climbed over the others. When the engine stopped, she lay on her left side beyond the siding. The cab was gone, the fireman was gone, but on my side of the run-board — at my very feet — lay the bodies of three little girls.

I tried to get up, but found that my right leg was held fast by one of the cab braces that had bent over and jammed it. The sounds that came from the wreck were appalling, — yells and groans in the shrill voices of women and children, with occasionally a deeper tone, showing where a man was. I did not know at first that I was hurt at all, but now my imprisoned leg began to pain me, then I felt a suffocating sensation within, as if a blood-vessel had been ruptured, and I was being drowned out with my own blood. My eyes became dim, my head swam, and I saw horrible sights.

To this day I don't know how much I saw and how much I imagined in the delirium that came over me.

The next thing that I knew I was in hospital, a "sister" bathing my forehead with cool water. I tried to ask where I was, but she told me to be quiet. It was a week before my wife was allowed to see me; she told me that over two hundred people on both trains had been killed outright, and many more than that injured.

When the wrecking-train was called, the roundhouse foreman, who was called to go with it, disappeared, leaving his job and family behind; and although we heard occasional rumors of his having been seen in various parts of the country, he never came back, and I do not think that his family ever heard from him afterwards.

As soon as I was able to be moved, the inquest was held. I told what I knew, which was little enough. The coroner asked me if I didn't know that the flanges on the leading wheels of the engine truck were worn dangerously thin; and I told him that both Frank and myself had reported them repeatedly, and that the foreman had promised me faithfully to turn the truck round on my return from the last trip; but as we had neither of us made a written report of the matter, and as the foreman could not be found, the company's lawyers objected to the admission of that item of evidence, and thereby enabled their employers to squeak out of a great deal of the responsibility, with which they should properly have been charged.

I had several ribs broken, and received internal injuries from the effects of which I have never fully recovered to this day. My fireman was killed, and his body completely dismembered, but no other employee on our train, strange to say, was at all severely injured. The baggage-master was found buried under a huge pile of heavy trunks, which had been piled to the roof on each side of the car; and although the car rolled over on its side, with the exception of a few bruises he was unhurt.

I was exonerated from all blame both by the coroner and the company, and ordered to report for duty as soon as I felt able to do so; but though I had never been the least bit squeamish over accidents before, this one took a strong hold on me. There were several families in the little town where I lived that had relatives killed and maimed in the wreck; and though I knew that I was not legally responsible, yet the thought that I might have prevented it, by refusing to take the engine out, tormented me so that I could hardly sleep nights. My appetite failed, and I became thin, weak, and nervous. Finally, during a conversation with my wife, I promised her never to touch a locomotive throttle again, and with one exception I never have. I had a talk with the general superintendent, and he tried to laugh me out of my resolution; but finding that I was determined, he advised me to take a month or two in the country and recuperate my nerves.

This I did, but on returning home I found that my antipathy to the road, and everything pertaining to it, was stronger than ever. I had another talk with my old friend, and after trying in vain to persuade me to return to work, he finally admitted that I would probably do better on another road where there would be nothing to remind me of the wreck. He asked me if I would like to go west again, and I told him that it was what I intended to do.

"Well," said he, "I may be able to help you a little; I have a brother-in-law who is general manager of the —— Railroad, and I will give you a letter to him; that will get you a job." And he did. He gave me a splendid letter, and procured the indorsements of the president and general manager. Armed with this formidable document, I bade adieu to my best of chums, Frank; and leaving my family under his care, once more set my face towards the setting sun.

On my arrival in St. Louis, I presented my letter, and was cordially received by General Manager ——, who asked what he could do for me in a manner that showed that he meant to do something. I told him that I should like a position as conductor, if he could place me. He thought a moment, and then said, "Passenger, of course?" "Preferably, yes, sir," said I. "Well," said he, "I think I will be able to fix you out in a very few days; we are just making out a new time table, and are going to put on a new through train; that will make a job for you. In the meantime, perhaps you had better go out and learn the road a bit."

To this I assented; and in less than a week I was a full-fledged passenger conductor. I was highly pleased with my new position. The pay was good, the duties were light, and for the first time in my life I had an absolutely clean job. When I saw the engineer, with his more or less greasy overclothes, crawling under his engine to try a wrench on eccentric bolts, and crawling out again with the sweat pouring down his face, I could not help saying to myself, "What a fool I was to do that so many years"; but I never let on to anybody that I had ever been anything but a conductor.

The life was uneventful, and therefore pleasant. I secured a cosy cottage within easy walking distance of the depot, had my family with me inside of two months, and everything ran along quietly with me for about two years. Frank had sold my house in the east, and took advantage of the pretence of settling with me to make us a very pleasant visit. Before his vacation expired, he received a notice that he had been appointed division master mechanic, and hurried home to enter upon his new duties.

Shortly after this I was called on my day off to take out a special, — a frequent occurrence, as the land speculators were in the habit of giving free excursions occasionally to prospective purchasers. It was a hot day; and when I went ahead to speak to the engineer and see if he was ready, I noticed that he looked flushed and warm, but paid no attention, as it was quite natural that he should on such a day. We had a little talk concerning the trains and where we had better sidetrack, and it was agreed that we would not be able to make more than ten miles before we would have to take the switch for the first inward-bound train. When the passengers were all on, I gave the signal, and he pulled out with a jerk, slipping his drivers in a way that was irritating to an old engineer like myself. Before we were clear of the yard, he was going at a forty-mile gait, and the cars were thumping over the frogs and switches at a great rate. I wondered what he was going so fast for, because we had plenty of time to get to the switch; and there was no possibility of our going any farther. When we struck out into the open country, the speed increased, until I remarked to the baggage-master that the engineer seemed to be in a devil of a hurry. Although I was not personally acquainted with the man, I knew that he was a regular freight runner, and should therefore have all the trains' times at his fingers' ends. But I couldn't help watching the road as we flew by, and wondering what he was running so for. I looked at my watch, made a rapid mental calculation, and decided that he was trying for the next siding, eight miles further along. If he kept up the gait that he was going, — and it was an open question whether he could or not, — he would reach the switch five minutes before the opposing train was due, which was not time enough; besides, a thousand and one things might happen to reduce his speed. And if the steam dropped five pounds, it would knock him out. What could he be thinking of, I wondered. We were within an eighth of a mile of the near end of the siding, and I pulled the bell; but he passed the switch without slackening his speed, and paid not the slightest attention to my signal. I stepped into the smoker and pulled the air-valve wide open that set the Westinghouse brakes, and brought the train to a standstill just as the last car cleared the switch. I told the rear man to open the switch, so that we could back in, and jumped down on the ground to give the engineer the signal. As I came in sight of the cab, he stuck his head out of the window, and shouted to me, in a thick, unsteady voice, which explained at once what the trouble was, "Say, did you pull the air on me? you —— ——" He called me everything but a decent white man. There was no time to blarney with him. I went back into the smoker and got the ventilator stick, which I concealed under my coat.

I then told the head brakeman and baggage-master that the engineer was drunk, and I was going to take charge of the engine, and back the train in; and I told the brakeman to come with me, and look out for the engineer when I should get him out of the cab; and I told the baggage-master that I would blow three short whistles when I got control of the engine, in case I found that I was unable to relieve the brakes, and in that case he should crawl under the cars and bleed them off. I saw that neither of them relished the jobs that I had set them; and I knew that by many of the men I was regarded as an interloper from the east, so there was a chance that they might be more than willing to see me stuck. However, this was a time for action, not words; so, calling to the brakeman to come on, I again jumped off, on the left side, and, shouting to the rear man to go back with his flag, I ran quickly ahead to the engine, where I could hear the engineer vainly attempting to release the brake, and cursing away to himself and the fireman as I stepped lightly up into the tender.

It is one of the unwritten laws of railroading that the conductor's authority ceases at the back end of the tender, and nobody had ever insisted on the rigid recognition of that law more firmly than I myself when I ran engines; so that I had every reason to expect anything but a pleasant reception. As I got up on the left side, neither of them saw me at first. The fireman was sitting on his seat,

"He nearly squelched the breath out of my body." — p. 297.

watching the engineer and idly ringing the bell, while the engineer himself was just in the act of pulling the reverse lever over, to "take the slack," hoping, no doubt, to be able to start her in spite of the brakes.

I let him get her in the back motion, and then seizing him by both shoulders, I settled back with all my might, dragging him from the foot-board down on top of myself. He was a big, fat brute, and nearly squelched the breath out of my body as he fell on top of me, the wet coal splashing from under us, as when a barrel is dropped into the water. It cost me a couple of minutes' hard struggle to turn him over, but, having done so, I didn't hesitate to give him a hearty rap with the ventilator stick which quieted him at once; then I looked for my valuable assistant. He was on the ground, looking on. "Get out ahead there and flag," said I; and away he went. Then, stepping up in the cab, I found, to my great relief, that I was able to let the brakes off from there, the air-pump having had time to get the pressure up while I had been arranging matters with the engineer; so, telling the fireman to get off and close the switch after me, I backed the train in and called my head flag. By this time, the engineer showed signs of returning consciousness; so I found a piece of bell-cord in the tank-box, and, calling on the baggage-master and brakeman, we tied him and put him in the baggage car. By that time the opposing train had passed, and I started the train. The fireman, who was not any too sober, here interfered, saying he wouldn't fire for "no brass-bound conductor!" My blood was pretty well up now, so I jumped down in the tank and argued with him for about three minutes in a manner that convinced him that his easiest way was to do whatever the "brass-bound conductor" told him to.

I stopped at the first telegraph office and sent back for an engineer. They sent me one, so that I only had to run the engine one way; but I was a sight for gods and men when I returned to the train. My coat was split up the back, and one sleeve torn entirely out. I was drenched from head to foot in the inky black water into which I had fallen in the tender; and had a bad cut in the back of my head, from which the blood had flowed copiously, contributing a variety to the otherwise sombre uniformity of my dirt.

The engineer was, of course, discharged; and the head brakeman, for having failed to assist me in capturing the engine, was jacked up for thirty days. As no one had seen the scrap between the fireman and me, and as he turned out to be a very decent fellow with a widowed mother to support, I omitted making any report against him.

CHAPTER XIX

CALLED TO THE GENERAL MANAGER'S OFFICE — IN CHARGE OF A BRANCH — PUTTING THINGS IN ORDER — FIVE YEARS' HARD WORK — BECOME GENERAL SUPERINTENDENT — ACCEPT A THIRD VICE-PRESIDENCY — GENERAL MANAGER — HANDLING A BIG STRIKE

A COUPLE of months after this, I was called to the general manager's office, and he asked me if I was a telegrapher. I told him that while I didn't pretend to be an operator, yet I had picked up enough of the art to be able to receive fairly good business. He said that was all that I should need, as there would be but little telegraphing to do where I was going. He then told me that the company had purchased a short road — about sixty miles long — connecting with another trunk line; and that, while they should probably run some main-line trains over it, as it had a fairly good business of its own, they should continue to operate it very much as it had been done heretofore, — with its own motive power and rolling stock. "From the way you conducted yourself when you found that you had a drunken engineer on the head end the other day," said he, "I am satisfied that you are a man who can successfully cope with sudden and unexpected emergencies, and those are just the kind of men that I like to have about me.

"Now, I am going to send you up there to operate that branch. You will receive general orders from this office, and we will let you know when we are going to send a train over your road; but as to the details of the operation, I shall leave that in your hands until I see whether you make a success of it or not. Of course, I don't want you to make any radical changes without letting me know about it beforehand. Your principal duty will be to build up the business of the road; it is fairly good now, but I am convinced that under the right kind of management it could be largely increased. You will make your headquarters at this end; and, for the present, you will have to do a great deal of the work yourself; that's why I asked if you were a telegrapher; but as soon as you make your road of sufficient value, so that we can afford it, we will give you more help."

I admit that I was not overjoyed at my promotion. It took me away from home altogether, and the prospect of being every man's jack, and working twenty-four hours a day, to say nothing of receiving more kicks than halfpence for my reward, was not alluring, especially when contrasted with my present easy and pleasant berth. However, we soon learn that railroads are not operated for the benefit of employees.

I found my little road in a most demoralized condition. The engines and cars were badly in need of repairs, and there wasn't an engine of the whole three that could go over the sixty mile division without stopping half a dozen times to "blow up." Nor was there a car, either passenger or freight, that had a full set of brake-shoes, and other things accordingly. The conductors had been running the trains to suit themselves, and as the conductor and engineer of each train lived near each other, their principal efforts had always been to get home at night, where they could lay over, train and all, until the next morning. There was a turnout about midway of the road, and as there could not be more than three trains on at a time, they easily kept track of each other, and all hands waited at the turnout until the arrival of the last train, when they proceeded on their way rejoicing.

The first thing I did was to send for machinists and material to get my engines and cars in order. I then made out a regular time table, consisting of one passenger and two freight trains; the passenger and through freight doubled the road every day, and the way freight went one way a day only. It wasn't a very satisfactory service, but it was the best I could do with the material at hand, and it was such an immense improvement over the former method, — which had been what railroad men call a tri-weekly service, *i.e.* trains go up one week and *try* to get back the next, — that the people along the line were very well pleased; for at any rate they knew now when they could get a train, or a car to ship their stuff in.

I had some trouble at first with the fossils who had been running on the road for years, and disliked my innovations; but after shifting a few of them out on to the main line, and filling their places with main-line men who knew no better than to obey orders, the rest recognized the fact that a new era had dawned on their little cross-country track, and governed themselves accordingly. The natural result of bringing order out of chaos was that the business of the road improved wonderfully inside of six months, and also that the operating expenses decreased proportionately.

During the second year of my incumbency, another passenger and two more freight trains were put on, necessitating the building of more sidings for passing points, and the little road flourished like a green bay tree. Although the general manager never said in so many words that he was pleased with my management, I felt satisfied that he was, for my requisitions for materials were always filled without a word of protest, and he voluntarily increased my personal staff until I was relieved from all manual labor, and was at liberty to devote my entire time and attention to the interests confided to my care.

I now began to experience that dignified sense of pleasure which comes to a man in authority, and wondered how I could ever have been so blind to my own interests as to have regretted giving up my train on the main line, to take charge of this branch.

I remained in this position nearly five years, and during that time great improvements were made on my little road. The company finally made a contract whereby all the coal for the use of their locomotives passed over the branch. This increased the business to such an extent, and I had to put in so many sidings, that I judged it would be more economical to double track the whole thing, and so represented to the general manager; but he was economically inclined, and though I showed him that it would have to be done in a few years, anyway, and that it was an unnecessary expense having engines and trains standing in side-tracks, waiting for an opportunity to go, he would not hear of it.

Our general superintendent left the road about this time to accept a position with an eastern road, and, to my infinite surprise, I was elected to the vacant position. I was doubtful about accepting, but the general manager called me to his office, and we had a long talk. He told me that he had nominated me for the place himself, because he had seen by my management of the branch that I had the trait which railroad companies value most highly; namely, managerial ability. He told me not to be frightened at the magnitude of the job, but to apply the very same talents to the superintendence of the whole road that I had so successfully employed in my management of the branch, and he predicted that I should be successful. At the same time, he assured me that I might depend upon his hearty coöperation, and told me always to come to him for any advice that I might need when knotty points presented themselves.

With such assurances of good-will and helpfulness on the part of my immediate superior, I felt emboldened to accept the position, with its largely increased responsibilities, and for four years I served under the immediate eye of my venerable friend.

He was one of the best railroad men that this country has ever produced, a perfect gentleman, and a true friend to me. I never knew him to hesitate a moment in giving his decision on any point, no matter how intricate it might be; nor did I ever know him to render a decision the wisdom of which after events failed to confirm. He could see farther, and more deeply and clearly, into a complex question, affecting innumerable interests, than any man I ever knew. His judgment — rendered almost instantaneously — seemed to be infallible.

It was due to my close connection with him for so many years that I owe what little ability I have.

After four years of apprenticeship and close study under this master mind, I had no hesitation in accepting the position of third vice-president and general manager of this road, when it was offered me.

On coming into the office, I found the road in rather bad shape, as compared with the one from which I had just come. There were abundant evidences of loose management, if not of peculation, and I proceeded at once to straighten out the tangle in which I found it.

The road had not been paying as well as its competitors for some time, and as a natural result investors were withdrawing their capital, and the stock was falling. To reclaim a property when it is in this condition and put it upon a paying basis is a big contract. But that was the condition that confronted me, and I determined to make a success of it, if it was humanly possible. The first thing to do was to stop all the leaks, curtail to the last degree the operating expenses, and inaugurate a system of the most rigid economy, without crippling the efficiency of the road.

For over a month I put in twelve and fourteen hours per day in my office, familiarizing myself with all the details of the road's business. I found that by adding slightly to the work of some of the men, I could dispense entirely with the services of quite a number, thereby reducing the operating expenses a small percentage.

I saw where a train could be advantageously taken off here and there, or two trains combined into one. I believed that by adding from one to five cars to some of the trains, I would be able to lay off a few locomotives and cabooses; and so on, all along the line, I perceived many places where little economies might be practised, which would foot up quite a respectable total at the end of the year. Still the results were not altogether satisfactory, and I was reluctantly obliged to admit to myself that a slight reduction of salaries would be necessary in order to accomplish the task I had set myself, of putting the road on its feet.

Knowing how unpopular such an act on the part of the management usually is, I tried to avoid it; but after looking the ground all over with the most careful scrutiny, I could see no other way out, and was in the very act of drawing up a reduced schedule of salaries, to be submitted to the president and board of directors with my report of the condition of the road, and my recommendations thereon, when I received word from my private secretary that a delegation of the employees wished to see me.

Although I was extremely busy, I ordered my clerks to pick up their papers and retire, for I have always held that the dignity of labor is entitled to the most prompt recognition.

They entered, four as fine, honest, bronzed fellows as you could wish to see; and as I looked over my desk at them, I remembered the time, years ago, when I had served on a similiar committee, and I sincerely hoped that they had not come to ask for anything that I should be unable to grant.

I bade them a cordial welcome, and asked one of their number to introduce the committee, which he did. They were an engineer, conductor, fireman, and brakeman; and they had come to ask for a ten per cent increase in their salaries. They had copies of the schedules of pay on several other roads with them, which showed a slight average increase over what we were paying. I let them talk themselves out; and then told them that I didn't think that the road was in a condition to increase salaries just at present. I reminded them of the poor business which the road had been doing for some time, but they said that they were not to blame for that; they had performed their duties faithfully, and were working harder if anything than the men on the other roads, who were getting more pay than they were, and so on, and so on; threshing the old familiar straw over and over again.

I finally told them that I would lay their request before the board of directors, but held out no hopes to them; they thanked me with rather poor grace and withdrew.

I now hurried up my report; the president called a special meeting of the board, and I laid it before them. I told them that as the men had asked for an increase of pay when a reduction was absolutely necessary to the existence of the road, they would probably strike when they received the notice. I argued that to be forewarned was to be forearmed, and guaranteed that if they would authorize me to spend a few thousands of dollars, I would not only defeat the strike, but equip the road with good men, who would be glad of a chance to work at the reduced rates, for I knew that in consequence of the recent failure of two large strikes there were plenty of good railroad men idle.

I had hard work to convince the board of the advisability of spending so much money for such a purpose, but having shown them that I could make up the sum in two months' difference in the rate of pay, they finally sanctioned the expenditure, and told me to go ahead.

I now knew that the crucial test of my ability confronted me. If I lost a strike, my position would very quickly follow it, and my prospects in life be forever damned; for the road was badly enough off now, and as it was by my advice that the strike was to be allowed to take place, it lay entirely with me to make it a success for the company.

For the next few days I kept the wires hot with messages to the general managers of all the roads in the country, asking for the addresses of good reliable men, whom they knew to have been out of employment long enough, so that they would be willing to accept employment in a strike. I soon had a list that would have manned the road twice over. I selected at haphazard twice as many as I wanted; and sent them a stereotyped letter, offering them employment, and stating frankly the conditions, and rates of pay; but guaranteeing them free transportation, and permanent employment for such as were selected, provided they proved worthy.

In nearly every instance the terms were accepted. I then wired to the several roads, requesting them to furnish the necessary transportation, and send the bill to us. They invariably furnished free transportation.

In the meantime, the committee called on me again and asked for the decision of the board. When I told them that it was found impossible to raise salaries at this time, they went away very much disgruntled.

I chartered a cheap hotel, and as fast as my men arrived I put them into it. When they were all here, the general superintendent and myself called on them, and picked out ten more crews than enough to man the road, and sent the rest home, grumbling that they had been swindled, and saying that they hoped I would lose the strike.

The next day I called a meeting of all my superintendents and gave them their orders. Each one was to be furnished with three more full crews than enough to man his division. They were to be given regular tickets, so that they could ride on trains without exciting the suspicions of the old hands, and were to be paid their wages while learning the road. Spotters were to be sent on the trains with them to see that they did not become familiar with the crews. Of course, they were to be lodged and fed at the company's expense; and some of them were so shabbily dressed that we had to buy clothing for them, so that they might not attract attention, or excite suspicion by continually riding in the passenger coaches.

At the end of one month the men all reported that they knew the road thoroughly. The next day I issued my notice of the reduction of pay; and, in order that it might not miss fire, I made it much heavier than I intended that it should be.

The committee called on me that afternoon. They were no longer respectful in their demeanor, but talked rather loudly. They asked me if I intended to starve them altogether. I told them that I had not thought of them at all. I said that the road could not afford to pay the wages that it had been paying, hence a reduction had been decided upon; but that it was not incumbent on them to accept it if they found it unsatisfactory, any more than it was incumbent on the road to pay them higher wages than its business would warrant.

"By G—d!" said the brakeman, "we won't accept it; we'll tie your d—d old road up — we'll strike."

"Strike, if you wish," said I; "that's your business."

"Yes, we will strike, you d—d old — "

Here I touched a button, and a couple of special officers entered and escorted the refractory committee out. The next day they struck; and the new men took the trains out nearly on time. On the third day the road was running as smoothly as it ever did; and I was continually denying myself to ex-strikers who desired to be reëmployed.

There were quite a number of the old hands who claimed that they had taken no part in the strike whatever; and therefore they thought that they should have been retained in the company's service; but I deemed it best for the morale of the equipment that none of the old men should be retained to cause heart-burnings and jealousies, so I let them all go.

With the exception of a few cases of drunkenness, burned boilers, and slight collisions, the new men did first rate. The superintendent soon weeded out the unreliable ones, and then they were as good as could be wished.

Six months later, the business of the road not having increased satisfactorily, I gave them another slight reduction; they accepted it in a proper spirit, and have never since asked to have their pay restored.

Within two years of my taking charge of the property the road was on a paying basis; and I flatter myself that to-day our stock compares favorably with the best in the market.

FINIS

www.ingramcontent.com/pod-product-compliance
Lightning Source LLC
Chambersburg PA
CBHW020235240426
43672CB00006B/534